The Book of
Honiton

Of Lace and Pottery Fame

GERALD GOSLING

HALSGROVE

Dedicated to the staff at Lisburne, past, present and future.

First published in Great Britain in 2005

British Library Cataloguing-in-Publication Data.
A CIP record for this title is available from the British Library.

ISBN 1 84114 408 8

HALSGROVE

Halsgrove House
Lower Moor Way
Tiverton, Devon EX16 6SS
Tel: 01884 243242
Fax: 01884 243325
Email: sales@halsgrove.com
Website: www.halsgrove.com

Title page photograph: *A Beer lacemaker, who helped to make Queen Victoria's wedding dress.*

Printed and bound in Great Britain by CPI Bath.

Acknowledgments

Without access to the considerable material available from the offices of the *Express & Echo* and permission to research the back numbers of *Pulman's Weekly News*, East Devon's leading newspaper, which has faithfully recorded Honiton's history for the past century and a half, this book would not have been possible and I must thank them both – especially Chris Wright, the archivist at the *Express & Echo*, and Philip Evans, the former editor of *Pulman's Weekly News*, as well as Tony Woodman, the present editor. Thanks also go to the Allhallows Museum, especially its curator, Margaret Lewis; the staff at Honiton Library; the Westcountry Studies Library at Exeter; Mr M.A. Smith, Honiton's town clerk in 2004; Mrs Cherie Batty, the Town Council office receptionist; Devon Army Cadet Force and Lieutenant Roy Poole and Staff Sergeant Helen Turner; and the constituency office of the East Devon Conservative Association.

Others who have allowed me to use their pictures or memorabilia are Les Berry, Colin Bowerman, Angela Browning MP, Pearl Carter, Sally Casson and the Honiton Working Men's Club, Mike Clement, John and Rosemary Connett, Arthur Dimond, Geoff Dibsdall and the Honiton branch of the Royal British Legion, not forgetting Keith Joslin, the Poppy Day organiser, and his welcome cup of tea, Paul Gosling, Richard Griffiths, Peter Harris, Peter Hayward, Jane Hedges, Peter Halse, Jim Kendall, Eddie Marks, Frank Martin, Les Moore, Doreen Newton (née Bambury), Jack Oakley, Adrian Pearson, Dave Pulman, Dave Rew, Jerry Rice and Sid Marks of Honiton Rugby Club, Margaret Robson, Gordon Sheridan, Beverley Spiller, Gwen Studley, Derek Yates, Brian Young and Honiton Golf Club.

Dr Terry Glanvill, Mayor of Honiton, is seen handing out certificates for those who 'beat the bounds' of Honiton in October 1972. Behind him is Mr Jackett with Audrey Hayman to his left.

Source Material

The titles listed below were the key sources used during the research and compilation of this book. If any reader is interested in finding out more about the subjects covered in this book, the author would recommend accessing the following titles in the first instance.

Arnold, Jacques, *History of Parliamentary Constituencies*, Patricia Arnold, West Malling, 2002.

Les Berry and Gerald Gosling, *Around Honiton in Archive Photographs*, The Chalford Publishing Company, Chalford, Stroud, 1995.

Cashmore, Carol and Collard, Chris, *The Honiton & Dorset Potter*, Anchor Brendon Ltd, Tiptree, Essex, 1983

Connett, John, *Honiton Borough Band Minute Book, 1936–41.*

Cox, Owen, *The History of Honiton Golf Club 1896–1996*, Square One Publications, Upton upon Severn, 1996.

Coxhead, J.W.R., *The Romance of the Wool, Lace & Pottery Trades in Honiton*, A. Dimond & Co. (Honiton) Ltd, Honiton, 1951.

Edmunds, M., *Honiton, an Old Devon Market Town*, West Country Books, Tiverton, 1993.

Farquharson, A., *The History of Honiton*, Devon & Somerset Steam Printing Company, Exeter, 1860.

Golesworthy, Maurice; Dykes, Garth and Wilson, Alex, *Exeter City, a Complete Record 1904–1990*, The Breedon Books Publishing Company Ltd, 1990.

Gosling, Gerald, *Exe to Axe, The Story of East Devon*, Alan Sutton Publishing Ltd, Stroud, 1994.

Kanefsky, John, *Devon Tollhouses*, Exeter Archaeology Group, Department of Economic History, University of Exeter, 1984.

Kendall, Jim, Honiton Royal British Legion Band Scrapbooks.

Pulman's Weekly News, various editions between 1860–2004.

Sheridan, C. Gordon, *Church of the Holy Family, Exeter Road, Honiton,* privately published, 1999.

The Devonshire Association, *Annual Reports and Transactions* for 1869, 1898 and 1939.

The swollen River Otter during 1970s flooding with Dumpdon Hill in the background.

Contents

Dumpdon Hill to the north of Honiton; it is the side of a late Iron Age earthworks and seen here in 1971.

THE
HONITON POOR'S RATE.

Extracted from "WOOLMER'S EXETER AND PLYMOUTH GAZETTE" for Saturday, 9th October, 1847.

A NOTICE was affixed to the Church Door on Sunday last, to the effect that the Magistrates had granted a Rate of *Two Shillings* in the Pound for the Relief of the *Poor* and *for other purposes*. The Rate-Payers of this Parish should certainly be informed why so unreasonably high an Assessment has now been made. It is not for the Relief of the Poor, and *their* attendant expenses solely, but comes (for some great portion of its Receipts) under the denomination of other purposes. What these *other purposes* are, we will now shew. Honiton in the earlier months of this year was made a Corporate Town, thereby destroying our Ancient Charter, and still more Ancient Offices of Portreeve, Bailiff, and Ale-Tasters, for those of Mayor, Aldermen, and Town Councillors. Of this we should not complain, provided the new order of things did not entail an expense, considerably beyond that of the old one ; and it is to meet PART of the expenses incurred in obtaining the Charter to constitute Honiton a Corporate Town, that the Rate-Payers are burthened with the extra amount of Assessment. The Town Clerk has issued his warrant to Mr. James Hussey, the authorized Collector of Rates for the Council, directing him to apply to the Churchwardens and Overseers of the Parish for the sum of £480, (the amount the Charter cost in being obtained,) £200 of which is to be paid by the 1st of NOVEMBER next, and the remaining portion by the 1st of MAY, 1848. In the above sum of £480, not One Penny is included for the Council's expenses of the current year.—It was generally understood that the Paving Trust would be dissolved, and thrown entirely over to the Town Council, as soon as they became Incorporated. That the Paving Trust has been nominally superseded by the Town Council, we cannot say. But why, if that Trust be dissolved, do the Council still continue to Collect the Quarterly Payments leased by the old Paving Trust? Can these be lawfully collected when there is, or is assumed to be, no such body ?—It is hoped that the Town Council will let the Rate-Payers know what Money they really receive from them, and Collect it by no other method than a Borough-Rate.

WOOLMER AND CO., PRINTERS, GAZETTE-OFFICE, EXETER.

Above: *Town councillors Ruth Robson (front), Ron Webb (centre), and Roy Coombes examining the waterwheel in the late 1990s; it was built locally in 1898 for the Old Mill in Mill Street that local residents want listed to protect for posterity as an important part of Honiton's history.*

Below: *High Street, Honiton, looking west, c.1850.*

Honiton in History

Now from the height 'midst scatter'd filds and groves
Our eye o'er Honiton's fair valley roves. – Gay.

Man settled in the area around Honiton long before the narrow confines of recorded history. Indeed, a few miles to the east Hembury Castle and its earthworks have sat brooding inexorably over the Otter valley since the fourth century BC; carbon dating of charcoal in a ditch there tells us that Neolithic man first made his home on the summit of the 884-foot-high hill in around 4200–3800BC.

Eight sections of that ditch go in a curved line from east to west across the middle of a later Iron Age fort. At the eastern Iron Age entrance a further section of the Neolithic ditch was discovered and traces of the side of a near-perfect circular hut was found near the western Iron Age entrance. In around 1800BC Hembury Fort was evacuated. Whether this was due to plague or enemy action is not known, but it remained empty for 15 or 16 centuries, until around 200BC when one of the Dumnonii tribes set up home there and built a single-rampart wall around the hill using materials from an inside quarry ditch. Later, two more ditches were dug to provide an outer bank and, in the Belgic period (2700BC–1700BC), two banks were built roughly halfway across the fort. This suggests that the northern section was used for cattle; the better-protected southern end was for human habitation. Stone Age man travelled from Hembury Fort to Beer Head, some 15 miles away, to work the cliffs there for flint to use for their arrows, spears and working tools.

Hembury is suggested as the lost Roman port or town of Moridunum. Be that as it may, the same claims are made for Seaton and both can be reasonably tailored into the known facts. Some experts point to the Celtic 'Mor-y-dun' (sea town) for Seaton; other experts prefer 'Mawy-y-dun' (great hill-fort) for Hembury Castle. Not even *The Fifteenth Itinerary of Antoninus* provides a lot of help. Antoninus records the mileage (Roman) from Calleva (Henley) to Isca (Exeter). Along the way he gives Moridunum as being 36 Roman miles from Durnovaria (Dorchester) and 15 from Isca. The distance from Dorchester to Seaton is approximately 36 modern miles. Hembury Fort is about 15 modern miles from Exeter, but that is in a straight line; via the old line of the Fosse Way (the modern A30) it would have been longer. It is known that the Romans did occupy Hembury for a spell and that there is considerable Roman building work at Seaton, where a tile was found of the Second Augustine Legion commanded by Flavius Vespasian who later became Emperor. Also, the Romans were

working the stone at Beer, near Seaton, soon after they arrived in East Devon. Take your pick but, as a Seatonian born and bred, I am probably biased.

Some 5 or 6 miles to the south of Honiton, Blackbury Castle is a smallish Iron Age fort on the top of a hill that looks out over the tiny hamlet of Southleigh. Blackbury Castle is oval in shape with one bank and a triangular annexe on the south side. A corn-drying area was discovered inside. Because Blackbury Castle is covered with trees at the time of writing, the ideal time to pay a visit is in early May when the bluebells simply carpet the entire fort and hedges for miles around. There is another Iron Age fort two miles north of Honiton on the top of the distinctive, 856-foot-high Dumpdon Hill. This one has double ramparts and is 800 feet long and 370 feet wide. The entrance is on the north-east and flatter corner and has an extra terrace outside for additional strength.

Also, away to the west in the Axe valley, a line of forts that run from Hawkesdown Hill, via Musbury Castle and Membury Castle, to Castle Neroche in the high Blackdown Hills above Taunton, marked the border between the Dumnonii and the Durotriges tribe that gave Dorset its name.

In 1934 a Bronze Age urn and calcified bones were unearthed at Honiton golf course during the construction of the 11th tee and the 12th green. They are in Exeter Museum in 2005. The golf course lies around 800 feet above sea level on at the north-western end of the Honiton and Gittisham Commons, an area with a considerable number of prehistoric tumuli. The most obvious one is near Putts Cross, where the Honiton–Sidmouth Road crosses the road to Seaton. In the past 40 years it has almost vanished beneath small trees. At the crossroad there is a stone on which human sacrifices were said to have been made and, according to local legend, the stone rolls down the hill during the night to the river in an attempt to wash the bloodstains away.

Honiton was never a Roman settlement, even if a later length of their Fosse Way runs arrow-straight through the modern town's centre. They may have placed a small post at the eastern end of the modern town where the old Icknield Way met the Fosse, but even that is not known for certain.

M. Edmunds, in *Honiton, An Old Devon Market Town*, puts the Roman road that runs from Dorchester via Bridport and Honiton to Exeter as the Fosse Way – in fact it is the Icknield Way.

Little is known of the town after that until the Saxons arrived around the beginning of the seventh century, their victory at Beandun (said to be Bindon above Axmouth) in 614 would have opened up the path into Devon and, despite advances made to the contrary, Honiton is an Old English name. Baring-Gould in his *Book of the West* felt that the name was Celtic, coming from their 'hen' (old) and there is the oft-quoted story that the name stems from the honey that was once plentiful in the area, especially at Blackborough, a few miles away.

Both theories are surely fanciful, as is the claim which states that the name comes from the French 'honi' or 'disgrace'. This claim also tells us that all the women in the parish were barren and a local priest told them to go St Margaret's Chapel to pray for a day and a night and, by means of a vision, they would all become pregnant. Those who favour this version point out the presence of a pregnant woman on the town's coat of arms. She is kneeling before an idol that has put his hand above her head.

A lovely story, but Honiton appears on old documents as, among other things, Honeton, Hunnington and Hinniton, and all three put in an appearance long before St Margaret's Chapel was even thought of.

No, Honiton is a Saxon settlement, as proved by the names of many of the farms dotted around the neighbouring countryside: Woodhayne, Woodhayes, Hutchingshayes, Holmsleigh and Shapcombe (sheep combe) to mention but a few.

Our first real picture of Honiton is given in the Exeter Domesday (1086), in which it was stated:

The Earl has a manor called Honetona, which Elmer held on the day that King Edward [the Confessor] was alive and dead, and it rendered geld for five hides. These can be ploughed by eighteen ploughs. Dreus holds this of the Earl. There he has in demesne two hides, and the villiens three hides and sixteen ploughs. There Dreus has 24 villeins, and six bordars, and three serfs, and two head of cattle, and four swine, and eighty sheep and fifty acres of wood, and eighteen acres of meadow, and of pasture one leuca in length and five furlongs in breadth, and one mill which renders by the year seven shillings and sixpence, and two salt workers who render by the year five shillings; and it is worth by the year six pounds when he received it.

For obvious reasons William the Conqueror's Domesday never mentioned the name of Harold II (one of the better English kings despite his short reign and his defeat at Hastings).

Excluding Dreus, his family and any retainers, there were 33 families at Honetona, which – at one husband, one wife and only one child only per family – gives a population of around 100 people, more if you include Dreus, which, I suppose, you must.

Given that most families would have had more than one child Honiton's population at the time of Domesday would have been between 150–200.

Perhaps it might be helpful to put some of the old words into modern-day English. Demesne was land attached to a manor and retained by the owner for his own use. A villein was an unfree peasant bound to his lord who, in return for the land, gave his lord services and dues, and a serf was one who was tied to working on his lord's estate, in other words almost a slave. A hide was the amount of land thought to be necessary to support a peasant household and allotted to every free householder. A leuca (or leuga) when describing length is equal to 12 furlongs.

The mention of two salt workers in Domesday is interesting. They were almost certainly two men who paid Dreus five shillings to rent saltpans on the coast near Honiton; they would have been at Budleigh (the 'East' came later), Salcombe Regis ('salt combe') or Seaton, where traces of the old saltpans can still be seen at the time of writing in Seaton Marshes and, like Honiton, was one of the many manors held by William, Count of Mortain.

The Count of Mortain was a cousin of Henry I (1100–35) and was also a grandson of Richard III, Duke of Normandy. The Count sided with Henry's brother Robert in the internecine squabbles that plagued Norman England. William the Conqueror left Normandy to the eldest of his nine children by Matilda of Flanders, Robert, and England to William II (1087–1100). He believed that Normandy was his by inheritance and should go to Robert, the eldest son, but England, his by conquest, could go to whichever son he wanted it to go to. Robert was bought off during William II's reign but with the powerful support of Anglo-Norman magnates such as William of Mortain, fought for his right to the English throne against Henry I (1100–35). The war dragged on until 28 September 1106, when Henry defeated Robert at the battle of Tinchebrai just a few miles to the north-east of Mortain on the rolling countryside above the infant River Vire. The actual site of the battle is not now known but on the crossroads as you enter the modern

An early print showing the Shambles in Honiton's High Street in 1705 if the date on the reverse is to be believed. The Shambles were pulled down in 1823, which would have made life much easier for the coach drivers, such as the one on the right.

Tinchebray from Mortain there is a plaque that tells you that it was nearby.

Duke Robert spent the rest of his life in prison, as did William of Mortain who was deliberately blinded as well. Henry gave the manor of Honiton to Richard de Redvers, first Earl of Devon, and it stayed in that family's hands until 1293 when it passed to the Courtenays.

The last of the Redvers was Isabella de Fortibus, Countess of Devon in her own right and a strong-willed woman as well. She had a row over the sale of fish with the city fathers at Exeter and built a weir below Exeter preventing ships from reaching Exeter, forcing them to unload at Topsham and pay the Countess for the privilege. To this day that part of Exeter near the weir is known as Countess Wear. The city took legal action, but to no avail – Topsham remained the port for Exeter, including the consider-able and lucrative woollen trade, until the seventeenth and eighteenth centuries. The construction of the Exeter Ship Canal between 1564 and 1567, the first lock canal built in England, did little to help.

Nearer Honiton, and probably apocryphal, Lady Isabella is said to have been asked to adjudicate when the good people of Honiton, Sidbury, Gittisham and Farway were unable to agree where their parishes met. Lady Isabella said she would throw her ring in the air and where it landed would be the exact spot. She did, and it landed in a mire that is known to this day as Ring o' the Mire.

Farquharson, in his *History of Honiton*, says that Honiton was created a borough by prescription in the 28th year of the reign of Edward I (1300); it certainly sent two members (Johannes de Swengethall and Galfridus Tolemer) for the first time to a parliament at Lincoln on January 20 the following year. But Honiton is listed in an Assize Rolle for Devon in 1228 as being among the 18 boroughs that sent burgesses to meet the justices in eyre. Eyre, also known as 'justices in itinere', which stems from the Latin 'iter' or 'journey', developed from the journeys that the King and his court made around England to deal with civil and criminal cases. During the reign of Henry II (1154–89), who was a great administrator, legal matters and work were vastly increased and Henry, unable to meet such an increase in courts in person, sent judges from his court 'on eyre' to deal with many legal matters in his place.

St Margaret's Chapel was originally founded in 1374 as a lazar-house for diseased persons, particularly lepers, the name being a biblical allusion to Lazarus, the name of a beggar covered with sores *(Luke 16:20)*. It was rebuilt as a hospital in 1530 by Thomas Chard, popularly supposed to have been the last Abbot of Ford Abbey, but claims are made that he was actually the Prior of Montacute. The hospital was re-founded in 1542 with five thatched almshouses, four more being added in 1801 with one occupant acting as the governor with a wage of three shillings (15p) a week. The others had a shilling a week and all received a Christmas bonus of ten shillings. In 2005 part of the original houses is now a meeting-place of the Jehovah Witnesses.

About two miles to the west of Honiton is Fenny Bridges where some of the last agonies of the Prayer Book Rebellion took place in 1549. A ragged army of Devon and Cornish men lined up in a field known as Fenny Mead, where they were sorely treated by a much-better-equipped army under Lord Russell. But, traditionally, Devon and Cornish men never know when they are beaten and they regrouped and came back for another go at the King's men. They lost 1,000 men in all.

The wounded were tended in the manor-house that was burnt to the ground as a reprisal. A further reprisal was carried out against the landlord of the inn (now called the Greyhound after the London coach that changed horses there). He had harboured some of the defeated army after the battle and was hanged, drawn and quartered outside his own inn. The Greyhound was virtually destroyed by fire overnight in 1968, but a replica was built four years later.

The rebellion had started as a protest against the introduction of the new Prayer Book during the minority of Edward VI (1547–53). Lord Russell had been forced into the battle at Fenny Bridges because the rebels blocked his path to Exeter, which was being besieged by a strong force under Humphrey Arundel and was in considerable danger.

After the battle Lord Russell retreated back to Honiton instead of heading for Exeter. The reason is said to be that the sound of church bells led him to think that the countryside was being alerted to join the rebellion. A further retreat was planned but Lord Russell plucked up his courage after the arrival of Earl Grey with a considerable number of reinforce-ments and headed towards Exeter where he defeated the rebel army at Bishop's Clyst.

One of the sparks that ignited the Prayer Book Rebellion had burst into flames near Bishop's Clyst at Clyst St Mary when Sir Walter Raleigh's father, another Walter, heard an old woman complaining about having the new Prayer Book forced on her and other people. Raleigh told her to shut up and grin and bear it. She rushed off to the parish church and

St Margaret's Almshouses, Honiton, in 1906.

9

Honiton High Street in 1745 with Allhallows Chapel tower in the background; it was burnt down during the fire of 1765 and is now the site of St Paul's Church.

told the congregation what Raleigh had said to her. In a few moments a lynch mob was rushing after him and he barely escaped with his life.

Royals who are known to have come to Honiton include Charles II who visited Thomas Marwood at Marwood House. This is the attractive house at the top end of High Street that was built in 1619 by John Marwood whose father, another Thomas, was physician to Elizabeth I, no doubt on the strength of his having cured her favourite, the Earl of Essex, when all other London doctors had failed. He was a good advert for his medical skills, dying at the age of 105 after practicing for 75 years. The second Tom's friendship with the King came because of his loyalty to the Royalist cause, which led to him being known as 'the loyal physician'.

It is said that an underground passage existed from Marwood House to Dumpdon Hill and it was claimed on a BBC programme in 1957 that there had been a door in one of the bedrooms on the Monkton side of the house that led on to a stone flat and then stone steps within the wall.

Earlier, Henry III called in at Honiton for a three-day stay during March 1230; his son, Edward I, was there in 1297 on his way to Lyme Regis; Catherine of Aragon passed through in 1501 on her way from Plymouth to London and her short-lived marriage to Prince Arthur, eldest son of Henry VII. Catherine later married Henry VII's second son, Henry Prince of Wales (later Henry VIII). In 1833 Princess (later Queen) Victoria waited inside the Dolphin Hotel while the horses were being changed. In April 2005 the Princess Royal visited Honiton.

In 1789 George III, his wife and three daughters, were entertained at Escot House by Sir George Yonge, the Secretary of State for War. Oliver Cromwell was at Ottery St Mary during the Civil War, wreaking considerable damage to that town's splendid church as revenge when the Ottregians refused to give any money. He would almost certainly have passed through Honiton on his way there.

Escot House was built between 1680–88 for Sir Walter Yonge of Colyton. In 1794 George Yonge sold it to Sir John Kennaway but, around ten years later, the

fine building was completely destroyed by a fire, thought to have started when the curtains in a dressing-room were set alight by a candle. Some 30 years later Sir John's son, another Sir John, rebuilt the house.

During its original construction some of the workers are said to have downed tools and gone off to join 'King' Monmouth on his way to Sedgemoor, and after the battle some were hanged at Talaton at a crossroads known as Bittery Cross. Fable has it that a ghostly horse and cart carrying the prisoners to their doom has been seen nearby. This is pure fable. As many as 23 rebels were tried at Exeter on 14 September 1685 for their part in the Monmouth Rebellion, 14 of them coming from East Devon, including Honiton. But they were hanged at Exeter, Crediton, Colyton, Ottery St Mary, Axminster and Honiton, no mention being made of Talaton. The four hanged at Honiton were Henry Knight, Samuel Pots, John Knowles and Thomas Broughton.

The memories of the grisly treatment handed out by Judge Jeffries were still fresh in the mind three years later when William of Orange landed at Brixham on 5 November 1688. Unlike Monmouth he brought a real army of around 20,000 men with him and the West Country greeted him enthusiastically. Nine days later he had reached Exeter, his advance guard reaching Honiton the following day. Meanwhile, King James II's support was haemorrhaging away, including John Churchill (later First Duke of Marlborough) who had just been appointed Lieutenant General by James. The advance guard was under Brigadier Tollemache who was soon joined by several of James's officers – so many that James declared that Honiton had seen the turning point in his fortunes and led to his flight to France. William of Orange became king on 13 February 1689 and was crowned as William III (1689–1702) in the following April, along with his wife and joint monarch Mary II (1689–1694).

Honiton received a good testimonial from Daniel Defoe, the author of *The Life and Surprising Adventures of Robinson Crusoe, Moll Flanders* and *Tour of the Whole Island of Great Britain*. The latter of the three books was written between 1724–27, Defoe calling in at Honiton to find that it was:

A one-pound note issued by the Honiton Bank on 28 October 1814.

... a large and beautiful town, very populous and well built, and remarkably paved with small pebbles that on either side of the way a little channel is left shouldered up on the sides of it, so that it holds a small stream of fine clear running water with a little square dipping place at each door... it is so much pleasanter and agreeable to look on than at Salisbury...

Mr H. Tapley-Soper, Exeter City librarian, wrote in 1913 that the town of Honiton:

... is of considerable antiquity, and was referred to in Domesday as the manor of Honetona, which was held by Elmer on the day on which King Edward (the Confessor) was alive and dead...

He went on to say that Honiton had not played any real part in national affairs except to mention that, during the Civil War, the Parliamentary army camped there for a night on its way from Chard to Cullompton.

But, unlike the Monmouth rebellion, the Civil War largely passed Honiton by, although troops did pass through the town. Prince Maurice and his men did stay there for a very short spell in 1643 and in 1645 Lord Goring and his men marched through the town in the dead of night. Goring had fought with Charles I at the Royalist defeat at Naseby in 1644 and then took command in the West Country. The day after Lord Goring passed through Honiton, Sir Thomas Fairfax, the man who had commanded the Parliamentarian army at Naseby, arrived there and stayed the night. Fairfax was one of Cromwell's

ablest commanders and, besides his success at Naseby, also fought at Marston Moor (1644) and was in command at the Battle of Langport (1645).

During the Commonwealth John Eedes, Rector of Honiton since 1614, was ejected in 1648. He died in 1651 and his successor, Francis Sourton, was deprived of the living in 1662.

The Devonshire Association first met at Honiton in 1868 under the presidency of J.D. Coleridge, Esq., (later the Rt Hon. Lord Coleridge F.R.S., Lord Chief Justice). It returned to the town in 1898, when Lord Coleridge was again president, and in 1939 and 1970. Oddly enough, in 1970 no paper was read about Honiton's past, the town's only mention in *The Report and Transactions of the Devonshire Association* for that year being in some general notes on *Late Roman Coinage in South West Britain*.

Honiton street market dates back to reign of King John and here in May 1990 Elizabeth Thurgood leads the dancers at a Honiton Medieval Market, held to bring back the spirit of Merrie England.

General Election results in Honiton were usually announced from the Dolphin Hotel. But they were also shown outside the police station in High Street as seen here in 1929. In older days successful candidates were chaired from the Market Cross, towards the eastern end of High Street, back to their headquarters. The result in 1929 was: Morrison Bell (Conservative) 17,911; Halse (Liberal) 16,353; Davis (Labour) 913. Of interest is the old police station, subsequently knocked down and replaced by a more modern building that stands some way further back from the road. The picture (right) shows the crowd waiting for the result outside the Conservative Committee Room.

Announcing the result for the Honiton constituency in the 1929 General Election from the balcony of the Dolphin Hotel. Although Labour had the most number of seats nationally they did not have a majority and had to form a minority government with the help of the Liberals. Major Arthur Morrison Bell won the Honiton seat for the Conservatives.

Chapter 2
Honiton's MPs

Mr Tapley-Soper admits that even if the town's political history is not all that exciting, it is, at least, interesting. I disagree. There is much to excite and engross the local historian in Honiton, not least the fact that it sent its representatives to parliament in the fourteenth century as well as from the mid-seventeenth century until the Reform Bills of the nineteenth century, when so much of the abuse that went on in such places as Honiton was swept away. At first freemen of the borough, who paid 'scot or lot', or, in plainer English, paid the poor rate or the church rate, held the franchise. The word 'scot' has its origins in the Norse 'skot' (shot), and it is reinforced by the Old French 'escot' (also related to 'shot'). Later, the franchise was extended to the inhabitants who could prove that they provided their own food and were masters of the hearth on which it was cooked, and controlled the entry to the dwelling. This right to a vote stems from the practice in medieval boroughs of occasionally eating in public to prove that one was a freeman rather than a serf.

It was, for many years, a pocket borough and for well over a century members of the Yonge family represented it. Other famous local families to represent the town included the Courtenays and Dukes. In more recent times Lord Cochrane (later Lord Dundonald) contested the borough. He did so at a by-election on 11 April 1806 and came fourth. He thoughtfully paid ten guineas (£10.50p) to all the 124 people who had voted for him (£1,302). That was a considerable amount at the time, and it was hardly money well spent. A subsequent election on 15 December of that year did see the noble lord on his way to Westminster, but he did not stay there for very long – another election was held on 22 June 1807 and he did not stand. He was not all that grateful and denounced Honiton as a rotten borough, and added rude words about the venality of its voters. 'The member who sat for Honiton,' he told the House, 'was like a man in a dirty shirt.'

Cochrane first went to sea in his uncle's frigate in 1793. In 1801 he captured a Spanish frigate when commanding a brigantine. Promoted to commanding frigates he led a fireship attack on the French fleet in 1811 and became a national hero. He certainly made a splash when he began campaigning at Honiton for the 1806 election. He arrived there on Whit Sunday in a carriage and four and was accompanied by many of the officers and men of his ship, the *Pallus*, a 23-gun frigate.

In 1814 Cochrane was sent to prison for fraud and, any further career with the Royal Navy seeming out of the question, he commanded Chile's fleet against the Spanish and then Brazil's fleet against the Portuguese. Coming back to Europe, he joined the Greek fleet and commanded a squadron against the Turks at the Battle of Navarino (1827). He was eventually reinstated in the Royal Navy and, no doubt, uttered some salty sea-dog language when, at the age of 80, he was turned down for action in the Crimean War (1853–56). Surely he is the most colourful of the 64 members to have represented the good (and bad) voters of Honiton. One of his second cousins is included among the 64 – Alexander Dundas Ross Wisheart Baillie Cochrane (surely the one with the longest name), who was Honiton's MP from 1865–68 and the last man to be elected by the town before it was disenfranchised.

The Yonge family of Great House, Colyton, who moved to Escot House, owned the Battishorn estate in Honiton and no less than six generations from father to great-great-great-great-grandson represented Honiton. Between 1640 and 1796, a period spanning 156 years in all, a Yonge was MP for Honiton for 127 of those years.

Other great families to represent the borough were the Poles and the Courtenays. The Courtenays came into the manor on the death of Hugh, second Earl of Devon, who died in 1377 and left Honiton to his third son, Sir Philip Courtenay of Powderham. As lord of the manor the Courtenays appointed the port reeve, the bailiff, the ale tasters, town crier and constables. The port reeve was once the magistrate of the court and the returning officer for the borough and, through his influence in appointing him, the lord of the manor could usually secure one seat for his protégé in a two-seat election such as Honiton's. Four members of the Courtenay family represented Honiton before 1574. In 1847 Joseph Locke bought the manor and sat as one of its representatives until his death in 1860. Locke had been articled as an apprentice to George Stephenson and had worked on the construction of the Liverpool and Manchester Railway. Halfway through his tenure he changed from being an avid Conservative into an equally fervent Liberal, with no apparent deterioration of his majority. After his death his widow sold the manor for just over £100,000 to Frederick David Goldsmid, a Jewish banker. No doubt it was meant to be an investment but Goldsmid died a year later (1866); his son Julian, who was returned unopposed in the

GENERAL ELECTION, 1906.

HONITON DIVISION.

Sir John Kennaway,

Your old and trusted friend for **35** years, asks for your

VOTE AND INTEREST.

Printed & Published by E. DIMOND, Honiton.

Sir John Kennaway, MP for Honiton from 1870 to 1910.

ensuing by-election, followed him but the borough was disenfranchised in 1868.

But it was the Yonge family who supplied the two most famous Honiton MPs – Sir William, who was elected ten times, and his son, Sir George, who was elected 12 times. Both men held five offices while representing Honiton. Sir William was, at various times, Commissioner of Revenue for Ireland, one of the Lords of the Treasury, one of the Commissioners of the Admiralty, Secretary of State for War and Joint Vice-Treasurer of Ireland. His son was a Lord of the Admiralty, Joint Vice-Treasurer, also Secretary of State for War, Master of the Mint and Governor of the Cape of Good Hope. Both men are buried at Colyton. Sir George Yonge was 'beggared by his constituents' but he did have a colourful time as Honiton's MP, including his first election in 1763, a by-election following the death of Henry Reginald Courtenay. His opponent was Anthony Bacon who, foolishly in a seat in Devonshire, supported the Cider Tax – foolish because Devon and Somerset would probably end up all square in any internecine war over which county made the best cider in the world. Premier Cru Chablis may be alright for 'Squire up at the Ouse', but when you had to do a man's work you needed a man's drink.

Men flocked into the town from all of Honiton's neighbouring villages. They did not have a vote, of course, but they fought Bacon's supporters at the drop of a hat and Sir George won by a convincing 224 votes to 120. Shortly after the by-election Sir George prepared a report on the Cider Tax for the govern-

ment and the tax was soon repealed. No wonder he was a member for Honiton from 1763–1802, although, in the end, his popularity vanished with his money.

Sir George often said that 'he had inherited an estate worth £80,000, had received another £80,000 with his wife, and a third £80,000 from his government appointments but that Honiton had devoured the lot.'

It was, of course, his own fault because he had no need to go on being a member in seven parliaments. It was sad that a man who served Honiton for 39 years as MP should not only be beggared by his constituents but, when he stood for the last time in 1802 without the money to bribe the electors, one of them spat in his face and another, a lady it is said, tried to burn his wig with a candle. He came third and bottom in that election, the votes cast being 73 for George Shum, 48 for Sir John Honywood and a mere 41 for Yonge.

Was it any wonder that Naimer, in his *Structure of Politics* in 1761, should claim that Honiton was one of the three most corrupt boroughs in England, along with Reading and Sudbury.

It was during Sir George's time as Secretary of State for War (1789) that George III and Queen Charlotte with three of their daughters were entertained at Escot. Later, his lack of money led to his selling the estate to Sir John Kennaway in 1802, and it was his grandson, another Sir John, who would become MP for Honiton for 40 years between 1870–1910. He was MP for Honiton from 1870–80 with Lord Courtenay, from 1880–85 with Sir William Walrond, and, after the number of MPs was reduced to one, on his own from 1885–1910.

THE FULL LIST OF HONITON'S MPS FROM 1301–11 AND 1640–2004

Honiton Town

20/01/1301	(at Lincoln) Johannes de Swengethall, Galfridus Tolemer.
08/08/1311	(at London) Johannes de Swengethall, Henricus Molend.
12/11/1311	(at London) Johannes de Honeton, Henricus Welych.
1640–53	William Pole, Walter Yonge.
	Charles Vaghan replaced Pole in 1646.
1654–55	Sir John Yonge.
1656–58	Samuel Serle.
1659	Walter Yonge, Samuel Serle.
1659–60	Charles Vaghan.
1661–79	Sir Courtenay Pole, Peter Prideaux.
1679–85	Sir Walter Yonge, Sir Thomas Putt.
1685–87	Sir Thomas Putt, Edmund Walrond.
	Putt's election was declared void but he won the subsequent by-election.
1689–90	Richard Courtenay, Edmund Walrond.
1690–1710	William Drake, Sir Walter Yonge.
1710–13	Sir William Drake, James Shepperd.
	A double return. James Shepperd was returned by inhabitants paying scot and lot, Sir Walter Yonge by the inhabitants in general; Shepperd was awarded the seat on 18 February 1711 on petition.
1713–15	Sir William Drake, James Shepperd.
1715–22	Sir William Courtenay, William Yonge.
	In a by-election in 1715 Courtenay was elected for Devonshire and was replaced at Honiton by Sir William Pole.
1722–27	Sir William Pole, William Yonge.
1727–34	Sir William Yonge, Sir William Pole.
1734–41	Sir William Yonge, William Courtenay.
1741–47	Sir William Yong, Henry Reginald Courtenay.
1747–54	Henry Reginald Courtenay, John Heath.
	Heath took the name of Duke after succeeding to the Otterton estates.
1754–61	Henry Reginald Courtenay, George Yonge.
	Sir William Yonge was also a candidate but he was returned for Tiverton.
1761–68	Henry Reginald Courtenay, John Duke.
	Courtenay died and a by-election on 22 November 1763 returned Sir George Yonge.
1768–74	Sir George Yonge, Brass Crosby.
1774–80	Sir George Yonge, Lawrence Cox.
1780–84	Sir George Yonge, Alexander McLeod.
	McLeod was unseated under the 1711 Act that required every borough member to possess an income of £300 per annum derived from land. In a by-election on 5 April 1711 Jacob Wilkinson replaced him.
1784–90	Sir George Yonge, Sir George Collier.
1790–96	Sir George Yonge, George Templer.
1796–1802	George Chambers, George Shum.
1802–06	George Shum, Sir John Honywood.
	Shum died and after a by-election on 13 March 1805 Augustus Cavendish Bradshaw was returned. Honywood died and after a by-election on 11 April 1806 Richard Batemen Robson was returned.
1806–07	Augustus Cavendish Bradshaw, Captain Lord Cochrane.
1807–12	Augustus Cavendish Bradshaw, Sir Charles Hamilton.
1812–18	Richard William, Howard Howard-Vyse, George Abercombie Robinson.
1818–20	Captain Hon. Peregrine Francis Cust, Samuel Crawley.
1820–26	Captain Hon. Peregrine Francis Cust, Samuel Crawley.
1826–30	Josiah John Guest, Harry Baines Lott.

1830–31	Josiah John Guest, Sir George Warrender.
1831–32	Sir George Warrender, Harry Baines Lott.
1832–34	Lord Villiers, James Russell Todd.
	Out of an electorate of 511 as many as 492 (over 96 per cent) voted.
1835–37	Colonel Hugh Duncan Baillie, Arthur Chichester.
1837–41	Colonel Hugh Duncan Baillie, James Stewart.
	Out of an electorate of 460 as many as 435 (over 94 per cent) voted.
1841–47	Colonel Hugh Duncan Baillie, Forster Alleyne McGeachy.
1847–52	Joseph Locke, Sir James Weir Hogg.
1852–57	Joseph Locke, Sir James Weir Hogg.
1857–59	Joseph Locke, Major Archibald Henry Plantagenet Stuart-Wortley.
1859–65	Joseph Locke, Alexander Dundas Ross Wisheart Baillie Cochrane.
	Locke died and after a by-election on 22 October 1860 George Moffat was returned unopposed.
1865–68	Frederick David Goldsmid, Alexander Dundas Ross Wisheart Baillie Cochrane.
	Frederic Goldsmid died and after a by-election on 4 April 1866 Julian Goldsmid, his son, was returned unopposed.

Honiton (Borough) was totally disenfranchised by the 1867 Reform Act
and a Honiton constituency covering East Devon was formed.

Honiton Constituency

1868	Sir Lawrence Palt.
1868–70	Sir Lawrence Palt, Lord Courtenay.
1870–80	Lord Courtenay, Sir John Kennaway.
1880–85	Hon. Sir John Kennaway, Right Hon. Sir William Walrond.
	Number of MPs reduced to one.
1885–1910	Rt Hon. Sir John Kennaway.
1910–31	Major Arthur Morrison Bell.
1931–55	Sir Cedric Drewe.
1955–67	Robert Mathew.
1967–97	Sir Peter Emery.

Sir Peter Emery in 1982, the last MP for the old Honiton constituency.

The town of Honiton and many of its surrounding villages were transferred to the Tiverton constituency which was renamed the Tiverton and Honiton constituency. The remainder of the old Honiton constituency was renamed as East Devon and the member from 1997 has been Hugo Swire.

Tiverton and Honiton

| 1997– | Angela Browning. |
| * Unopposed | |

All the Parliaments held after 1640 sat at Westminster except in 1681 when it sat at Oxford.

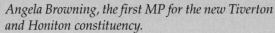

Hugo Swire, the first MP of the new East Devon constituency since 1997 when Honiton was transferred to the freshly named Tiverton and Honiton constituency.

Angela Browning, the first MP for the new Tiverton and Honiton constituency.

Chapter 3

Great-Grandad's and
Edgar William Pulman's Honiton

Although we might hardly recognise it as such, the Honiton of the mid-nineteenth century was a pretty compact and self-serving town and is described in *White's Devon Directory* for 1850 as having:

Union [workhouse], a Polling and a County Court District and a Petty Sessional Division, the latter consisting of the 18 parishes of Awliscombe, Branscombe, Buckerell, Comb-Rawleigh, Cotleigh, Dunkeswell, Feniton, Gittisham, Honiton, Luppitt, Monkton, North and South Leigh, Offwell, Upottery Widworthy and Yarcombe, for which the county magistrates hold petty sessions here monthly at the King's Arms Inn. The Mayor and ex-Mayor are magistrates for the borough.

The Market House, for the sale of Corn, cheese, butter, poultry etc., is in the centre of the town, and over it is a large Public Room. The late Paving Trust Commissioners, at a cost of more than £2,000, built it about 25 years ago. The market, held every Saturday, is extensively served with corn, cattle, and all sorts of provisions, especially of butter, of which great quantities are sent to London. Two great markets for cattle etc. are held the second Saturday in April, and the Saturday before the 18th of November, and a large annual fair on the Wednesday after July 19th. The gas works were commissioned in 1835, at the cost of £2,700, raised in £25 shares and the consumers are supplied at the rate of nine shillings [45p] per 1,000 cubic feet.

That Honiton was self-serving is underlined by the fact that, in addition to all the butter, eggs, meat and other farm produce available on market days, there were ten bakers, 13 butchers, and 16 shopkeepers, many of them grocers or connected with the grocery trade. A further 12 were actually listed as grocers, but five of which sold only tea. There were also five confectioners, eight milliners and 11 tailors, five of which were also drapers, in Honiton.

A total of 23 inns and taverns were listed: Anchor Inn, Angel, Black Lion, Carpenter's Arms, Chopping Knife, Crown and Sceptre, Dolphin Hotel, Exeter Inn, Fountain, Golden Lion, Green Dragon, King's Arms, London Inn, New Inn, Red Cow, Star, Swan, Three Tuns, Turk's Head, Vine, White Hart, White Horse and White Lion. There were also several beerhouses that held a licence to sell only beer and were often run in conjunction with another business. And, if all those places of liquid refreshment, along with three wine and spirit merchants and the off-licences found in

Honiton Borough Police shortly after the Borough Police Act (1856) required boroughs to have a regular police force. The sergeant lived in a cottage out of sight on the right, the men are pictured in the garden behind the old police station.

many of the grocers' shops, gave you a king-sized hangover, there were also five chemists to supply you with their various cure-alls. And if they could not cure you there were also six surgeons (doctors) who could.

Among the banks was the National Provincial Bank; it became the National Provincial Bank in 1924, was taken over by the National Westminster Bank in 1968 and is, of course, in 2005 better known as the NatWest.

Banknotes bearing Honiton's name were issued there, a proof £5 note being sold for £220 at Spinks in 1995. It featured a portrait of William IV (1830–37) and was dated May 1885 in ink.

In 1850 memories of the great fires of the eighteenth century were still fresh in the Honitonian mind. No less than 15 fire and life insurance companies had offices in the town.

There were also two auctioneers (Richard Frost and Richard Salter), six blacksmiths, three cabinet-makers, three coopers, three millers, two dyers, four gardeners, three hairdressers, three hop merchants (and two maltsters), two ironmongers, 13 lace manu-facturers, 11 masons (one of whom, Francis Hooper, also ran a beerhouse), eight painters, plumbers and glaziers, eight (yes eight!) straw-hat makers, three tinners, two turners and three watchmakers.

Edgar William Pulman's Honiton

Edgar Pulman, who was born in Luppitt on 20 August 1908, came to live in Honiton in 1912 when he was four years old. In November 1989, at the age of 81, he began writing his memories of the Honiton of his childhood and the changes that had taken place in the town since 1912; his *opus magnum* was finished in eight months and it is a remarkable piece of work running to almost 30,000 words. It is of immense value to students of the town's history and I am privileged to have his son David's permission to reproduce extracts from it here.

Mr Pulman's father opened a building business in Northcote Lane when he moved to Honiton in 1912; formerly Mr A.E. Dodd had occupied it, before he moved to Newlands. Edgar's first memories are of the building of the swimming-pool for Allhallows School (that has since been filled in) and the old Honitonians' club in 1913, the work being done by Charles Turner who had a builder's yard at West End.

Starting at the top end of High Street he takes the reader all the way around the town, giving an almost house-to-house description of not only the houses and shops but also of the people who lived or worked in them. Space dictates that I have quoted from the items that I feel will be off most interest to readers.

I was interested to read about Plympton House, the residence of Dr Hedden in the 1920s. It was for many years the residence of Charles Parsons Slade, a corn merchant, and after his death was home to his son Jimmy (my former employer). He ran the shop and stores in partnership with a Mr Yates. Next door was the old cinema owned by Mr H.R. Harris; these were the days of the silent films, and the show stopped between each reel as the projector could only take one reel at a time. The projectionist was Albion Wyatt and his son Jack assisted him. A pianist played music and one of them was Tommy Vincent, who was blind and, because he could not see the film, he often played music that was not appropriate to it. When Mr Harris retired in 1930 the business was taken over and the first 'talkies' were shown around that time. Mr Harris owned the cottages at the rear of the cinema and they were known as Cinema Row.

The first landlord Mr Pulman remembered at the Angel Hotel was a Mr Knowles. After his death it was taken over by Ralph Sprake who had spent some time in Canada. He ran a garage and repair shop in the yard and also ran a taxi service. The town's fire-engine was kept in the yard, Mr Sprake being the captain of the brigade.

Mr Pulman reminds us that the Dolphin Hotel was well known and popular in the old coaching days. The Banfield family owned the hotel for a great number of years, the last member of that family to be the landlord being Harry Banfield. A Mr Richards and then a Mr Fitch, who spent a large amount of money on the hotel and built the new ballroom between 1922 and 1923, succeeded him. Before it was built, dances and concerts were held in what was known as the

Assembly Room, which was situated over the old Pannier Market. The man in charge of the off-licence was Mr Pridam and you could buy a bottle of whiskey for 12 shillings and six pence (62p) at the time. In Mr Banfield's time he kept horses and carriages for hire and had a horse-drawn hearse. He also ran a horse-drawn bus to and from the railway station, which for many years was driven by William Norman.

At the top of Northcote Lane was a small inn called the Dolphin Tap that was used by many of the older locals, most of them crib players. During the Second World War it was patronised by the Home Guard and was always visited after a parade or drill (probably on the grounds that it was the nearest to the Allhallows Playing Fields where the Home Guard drilled). It is now gone and was used as a kitchen of the Dolphin Hotel until that part of the hotel was sold.

The Pannier Market adjoining the Dolphin was used on Saturdays for the sale of vegetables, butter, cream, eggs and other foodstuffs, and was also used to house the market stalls used in High Street. They were brought out on the morning of market day and returned in the evening. Also kept there was the steam-driven fire-engine. During the carnival the Pannier Market was used for skittles and there was a boxing ring for local contestants. To name a few boxers: Trooper Bowden, Seaman Proll, Joe Furneaux and Henry 'Bung' Chown. On the left-hand side of the central opening was the office of James Slade, the corn merchant who had his stores at the old butter factory at Littletown previously owned by Salter & Stokes of Chard Junction. The entire area was developed but the butter factory was bought by the Plymouth Brethren and rebuilt as a gospel hall in the 1980s.

Pulman, in his memories, recorded:

Just below the Pannier Market are the Vine Passage and the Vine Inn that has been in existence for as long as I can remember. Some of its landlords were Fred Richards, Bill Hooper and Harold Manley. Bill Hooper later took over the Red Cow and was followed by his son Kenneth. There is a large cellar under the Vine, and this used to get flooded to near its brim. The fire engine pumped this out on several occasions but I understand that they found the cause of the flooding and it no longer occurs.

The Drill Hall in King Street was once a large garden owned by Mr Archie Hoskins. After he sold it the Drill Hall was built along with a small bungalow at the rear to accommodate the Sergeant Instructor; it has since been demolished. The Territorial Army, very strong in Honiton at one time, used it for their drill and other activities and it was also the headquarters of the Honiton Miniature Rifle Club that had a large member-ship. The range was on the left of the main hall and members shot at 20 yards. The car park next to the drill hall was once the garden of the Star Inn.

Henry Proll, a haulier by horse and cart by trade, had

the contract to haul coal from the station yard to the gas works. He was also a farmer owning ground at Round Ball and he owned the Fair Field as well. The Fair Field was the site of the annual Pleasure Fair for many years, Circuses were held there and many of the fair people came back year after year with their pastimes such as the Helter Skelter, the Round-Abouts, the Gondolas with their wonderful fair organ, Hoopla, side shows and Nougat and Ginger Bread stalls.

There were many sideshows and fortune-tellers and there was always a boxing booth; Sam Mackowen ran one in particular. He was himself a good fighter in his younger days and he had two sons who were useful with their fists.

The boxers belonging to the booth would stand outside waiting for a challenge from someone in the crowd. There was one Welsh heavyweight by the name of Gypsy Daniels, a very well built man who had been with the booth for some time. Any challenger was offered thirty shillings [£1.50] if he could go three rounds with his opponent. Someone in the crowd who looked no more than middleweight once challenged Gypsy. I paid my shilling to see the fight and, soon after the fight had started a stranger in the crowd asked me if I knew who the challenger was. I told him that I did not and was told that he was young Freddie Mills from Bournemouth. The name meant nothing to me, but he so impressed Sam Mackowen that he travelled with the booth for some time. Later, of course, he went on to be World Champion at his weight.

Some years after the field was closed as a Fair Field the annual fair was held on several different sites. The Devon Lady portable building factory was built on part of the field but it closed and much of the old Fair Field has been built on, together with a garage and a builder's yard.

Our bathing pool was in the River Otter at the bottom of one of the fields and was known as Head Weir. The school now covers most of the fields and our bathing pool is now on the other side of the bypass in what is now called School Lane. It was a rough and muddy track used by cattle. It was the intention of Mr Middlemist, the head master of Allhallows School, to build a new school on this ground, and I understand that he purchased the farm for this reason. However the governors did not agree because Rousdon Mansion was on the market and the school moved there instead.

After Allhallows School left Honiton, the playing fields were purchased by the Borough Council, Mrs Phillips and Mr Frank generously giving towards the purchase. Cricket and rugby were played there for some years and then the cricket club was transferred to Ottery Moor Lane. The field is in very bad state [1989] and only rugby is played there now. The cricket pitch has gone and it used to be one of the best in the county.

Harry Aggar was the groundsman as well as being the Sergeant Major in charge of the Allhallows O.T.U. He went with the school to Rousdon but came back to Honiton when he retired. He first came to Honiton in 1917 after being wounded in the first [World] war. The grass of the playing field used to be cut by a horse-drawn mower; the horse was supplied by Mr Durbin and led by one of his employees, Mr Baker. After some years the school purchased a Dennis motor mower. Local horse owners collected all the grass for feeding purposes.

HONITON'S CENSUS RETURNS
1801 – 2,377
1811 – 2,735
1821 – 3,296
1831 – 3,509
1841 – 3,895
1851 – 3,427
1861 – 3,301
1871 – 3,464
1881 – 3,358
1891 – 3,216
1901 – 3,271
1911 – 3,191
1921 – 3,093
1931 – 3,008
1941 – no census
1951 – 4,613
1961 – 4,718
1971 – 5,027
1981 – 6,567
1991 – 8,988
2001 – 10,598

Honiton historian, the late Edgar William Pulman and his wife Doris on the occasion of their golden wedding anniversary in the 1980s.

The Round Ball Hill Rifle Range in 1905.

Above and below: *The 1909 Empire Day celebrations at Honiton included patriotic speeches from the men on a platform in the middle of High Street. The second picture (below) was taken later in the day, if the size that the crowds had grown to is any guide.*

Honiton's mayor, Alderman Tom Steel, seen as guest of honour at a Passing Out Parade at Heathfield Army Camp in 1965. Mrs Steel is in the centre.

Chapter 4

The Twentieth Century and Two World Wars

The Honiton Working Men's Club is first mentioned in 1906, although it almost certainly existed at least as early as 1893 as the Honiton Club and Reading Rooms in New Street, with Mr H.N. Pope as its secretary. In 1906 it was called Honiton Workmen's Club and it stayed as such until 1939 when it became Honiton Working Men's Club. The link with the Honiton Club and Reading Rooms is more than tenuous – during the years before and after the First World War it was often referred to as Honiton Workmen's Club and Reading Rooms.

During the very early years of the Edwardian era the club moved to the High Street where it stayed until 1968, when a move was made to the club's present home at Allhallows Court in Silver Street.

Until 1907 almost every town that held a market did so in one of its main streets where, from time immemorial, markets flourished and people went about their business without so much as a thought of the horseless carriages that were to come. By 1907, however, the age of the motor car had arrived and vehicles were proving a nuisance as they tried to thread their way through High Street. But it was a growing awareness of the importance of hygiene rather than the increase in motor vehicles that led to the Board of Agriculture laying down new requirements and moving street markets to permanent, purpose-built sites. Most such moves took two or three years to come about.

At Honiton the generosity of Squire Marker led to the acquirement of a new site close to the centre of the town. Prior to that the market had been held in High Street where space was left for the passing of horse-drawn vehicles including, among others, those of the Royal Mail. Mr Marker's generosity included payment for all the necessary building as well.

The new market was about an acre in size and had two entrances, one for sheep, and the other for cattle, pigs, and horses. The cattle pens had two enclosed passageways that led to the sale rings, which were occupied by the two local firms of auctioneers – Messrs Wright & Johnson (of Honiton and Ottery St Mary) and T.D. Hussey & Son (Honiton). Thus, the stock, when passing to and from the pens and rings, did not have to pass through the buyers or spectators. Sloping ways were built for loading pigs into the carts and two long sheds were built for cows and calves. It almost goes without saying that a weighbridge was provided.

Separate offices, rostrums and sale rings were provided for the two firms of auctioneers and, in addition, a central office next to the weighbridge was built for the market bailiff. The entire layout was specially designed to allow for any future expansion. Water was provided for all stock and also for washing down the premises.

In 1909–10 Mr J.J. Hardy, agent of the manor of Honiton, designed the market and Mr R.G. Spiller of Chard was the contractor responsible for the work.

Naturally there were many words spoken before the first market to be held at the new site on Saturday, 8 October 1910, got under way. The squire was there to trace the history of Honiton market that, he said, had been started in the reign of King John (1199–1216). Mr Marker was thanked by the mayor, Cyril Tweed, who told those present that he was proud to have served as mayor at a time when the town had received three great benefits – the abolition of the tolls, the introduction of the telegram service, and the opening of the new market.

Like today's public, the two auctioneers knew the advantage of advertising in *Pulman's Weekly News*

Opening of the new extension at Honiton Working Men's Club in 1982. Left to right, back row: *Derek Evans, Chris Pinnuck, Dr Terry Glanvill, Pat Evans, Ron Wilson;* front: *Mrs Pinnuck, Alex Gigg.*

Honiton Market on 15 May 1970.

Members of Honiton Working Men's Club at a 1980s function.

Left: *The Honiton Working Men's Club's crib team that won the Honiton Crib League's Cup in 1978/79.*

Honiton Working Men's Club committee in the 1950s.

Monsieur Henry Delisle inaugurates the naming of Avenue Mézidon-Canon off Church Hill in Honiton, c.1977. Left to right: Dr Kath Glanvill (Mayoress) *Madame Alice Delisle, Monsieur Henry Delisle (Maire de Mézidon-Canon),* Derek Eagles (behind), *Derek Yates (chairman of Honiton Twinning Committee) who is translating for Dr Terry Glanvill (Mayor of Honiton). Behind Dr Glanvill is the builder of the avenue.*

The Allhallows School Officers' Training Corps (OTC) on the shooting range, 14 July 1914. This date was roughly halfway between the assassination of Archduke Franz Ferdinand, heir to the throne of the Austrian-Hungarian Empire at Sarajevo, the 'Spark That Set The World Alight', and that Empire's declaration of war on Serbia that started the First World War.

A visiting officer addresses members of the Allhallows OTC (Officers' Training Corps) after their annual inspection. The inspection took place on 14 July 1914, exactly three weeks before the First World War burst upon a still largely unsuspecting Britain.

and both were a more-or-less permanent feature on the front page, where they not only gave details of what they would have on offer at the next market, but also of the many farm and house sales that took place in the neighbourhood.

After Lord Haldane's army reforms of 1908, public schools and universities were asked to form units of the Officers' Training Corps (Allhallows had one such OTC) and other Cadet Corps were formed into open units for boys who had left school. Many of them would serve in the First World War that started on 4 August 1914. Great Britain entered the First World War after Germany broke a treaty that both it and Great Britain had signed guaranteeing the neutrality of Belgium. The German army marched through that little country occupying all but a tiny corner of it to the north of Ypres, and as far as the coast at Nieuwport, where King Albert and the gallant Belgian army occupied the line to the left of the BEF (British Expeditionary Force) for the next four years.

The outbreak of war saw Honiton Cricket Club cancel all its remaining matches, but more important to some people was a letter from Captain Morshead, (commanding the Honiton Territorials) to the Mayor, Alderman R.H. Matthews, saying that Lord Kitchener had prohibited cigarette smoking in the Army and that several of the men were without pipes. The gallant captain asked the Mayor if the people of Honiton would like to supply 85 pipes. It was reported in *Pulman's Weekly News* that, 'The Mayor placed the matter before several of the inhabitants and the requisite number of good brier pipes were quickly obtained and sent to the Territorials.'

The Voluntary Aid Detachment (Devon 24) were already standing by after receiving a visit from Mr Davis, the county director, accompanied by Lady Fortescue, the president of the Devonshire Voluntary

Aid Detachments (VAD). Mr Davis expressed his satisfaction and highly praised their readiness. He could not say for sure if there would be a hospital at Honiton but that they should hold themselves in readiness to receive 50 wounded at short notice, at any time in the near or distant future.

A convalescent hospital was established in a building on the opposite side of High Street to St Paul's Church with Dr Steele-Perkins as the VAD's medical officer. Needless to say, the wounded soldiers were well treated by the town's people and, during convalescence, were visited with gifts and invited out for meals and car drives.

The appeal for recruits to bring the 4th Battalion Devonshire Regiment up to full strength for foreign service resulted in 35 men leaving for camp on 4 September. The party was made up of 23 national reservists and 12 recruits. They fell in at the Drill Hall and, after being addressed by the mayor and the rector, marched to the station led by the local Boy Scouts and their band. The station was crowded and the train left Honiton to the sound of 'Rule Britannia'

The Voluntary Aid Detachment (VAD) ran a hospital in Honiton's High Street during the First World War, where they cared for the wounded soldiers and sailors. Their medical officer was Dr Steele-Perkins.

Honiton Territorials pose at the station in September 1914 before departing for service in the First World War. The right picture shows the crowd that gathered to wave them on their way.

and the discharge of fog signals. A further 26 men had already volunteered to join the Honiton National Reserves and serve either at home or overseas. They were able to practise at an air-rifle range that was opened at the Globe Inn by the landlord, Mr Isaacs, and they guarded railway bridges until this job was taken over by the military. Then 25 of the men left for Salisbury Plain to join the Devonshire Regiment.

It was not all one-way traffic – Honiton had been selected as a training centre for 500 soldiers and 250 of them arrived in October when all the public buildings and unoccupied houses were secured for them, including the YMCA and the schoolrooms of the Baptist church.

The great and patriotic shout that went up a few days into the war was that it 'would be over by Christmas'. But there would be four wartime Christmases before the Armistice in 1918. The first of them found Honiton geared up to raising money for comforts and patriotic funds. The members of the Devonshire Regiment that were stationed in the town, and those who were unable to go home on leave, were not forgotten – they had a dinner of turkey, chicken and game with Christmas pudding and cream. The inmates at the Honiton Union only got roast beef. The soldiers marched to a special morning service at St Paul's and attended concerts during the next three days.

Honiton contributed to the war effort in many ways, other than sending its sons to fight. Children were given days off in the autumn to collect conkers (horse chestnuts), which, it was said, were used in the making of explosives, and sphagnum moss which was used to dress wounds and was usually taken to the station and handed direct to the hospital trains. There would have been a good crop of conkers in High Street itself from the handsome chestnut tree that still stands towards the eastern end of High Street at the time of writing – it appears in a picture dated 1879, which makes it well over 150 years old. But Honiton's biggest contribution to the war effort can be found in the 66 names that can be seen on the

war memorial. The Second World War saw only 22 names added, exactly a third. No wonder our grandfathers' generation called it 'The Great War'.

It was the end of that great loss of life that, when news of the signing of the Armistice reached Honiton, caused the town to almost vanish under a sea of flags and bunting. Excited crowds gathered in High Street cheering and singing patriotic songs. The pupils at Allhallows School and many other children rushed to the Allhallows Playing Fields. A number of German prisoners of war had been working there for some time under the charge of a Mr Rowland, removing a large hedge and some trees that divided the fields. A chorus went up from the children that an Armistice had been proclaimed, and this carried on for some time until the prisoners appeared to understand and were as pleased as the children. They were stationed at Combe Raleigh in a house named the Abbots and were hired out for work on local farms. Oddly enough, Abbots, built on the site of an earlier building in 1790, had a connection with the Second World War as well – a Colonel James lived there, whose nephew was Lieutenant Clifton James of the Royal Army Pay Corps and doubled as Monty in a successful attempt to make the Germans think that the Second Front would be opened in the Mediterranean theatre.

Although the First World War officially ended in 1919 when the terms of the 1918 Armistice were ratified, there were still trouble spots that owed their origins to aspects of the 'Great War'. One was Mesopotamia (now Iraq and still troubled) where Honitonian Captain John Reginald Howard Tweed, MBE, of the 94th Russell's (Indian Army) was awarded the Military Cross in late 1921 for heroism and leadership against 500 insurgents.

The first peacetime Town Council election in 1920 was restricted to the St Paul's ward and, for the first time in a municipal election, motor cars were used to convey voters to the polling booths in the town. It seems to have been of value, as the three retiring councillors, Messrs Foale, Payne and Otton, issued a joint address and poster. A fourth candidate was Mr A.P.

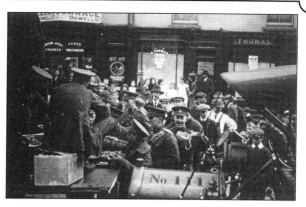

Above: *Soldiers from the Devonshire Regiment take a break for a meal in Honiton's High Street during the First World War. Judging by the direction the mobile kitchen and the vehicle to the right are facing, the troops are probably heading towards Salisbury Plain.*

Above: *A convoy of Canadian soldiers passing through Honiton's High Street during the First World War; it is possible they are returning to camp after practice at the firing range.*

Right: *New Street during the First World War with the Sun on the left; one can date it to the 1915–18 period because of the convalescing soldiers outside the inn.*

Members of 14 TD RAF Indian Force pose for their picture, presumably at a function (or reunion) in this country. Judging by the use of the RAF name the picture was taken after 1 April 1918, when the Royal Flying Corp became the Royal Air Force. The man third from the left in the back row is A.F. Studley, mayor of Honiton in 1942 and 1943.

Above: *Convalescing soldiers at Honiton during the First World War.*

Honiton Territorials with their machine gun. In the back row, Private W. Cann is second from the right and Sergeant E. Dimond is fourth from the left.

Below and right: *VAD nurses at Honiton during the First World War. Mrs Duncan is the tall woman in the back row, Dame Porter is the lady with the medals in the middle row, Mrs Stamp is second left in the front row with Miss Dunning on her left; second from the right at the back is Miss Marker of Combe House, Gittisham. In the second picture (right) Dame Porter and some of the nurses seen in the first picture are pictured with what appears to be naval convalescents bedded down on the floor of Allhallows Chapel.*

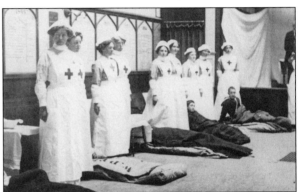

Moore, the ex-Servicemen's nomination. Moore had two cars bringing the voters to the booth and he came second with 292 votes – only eight behind Mr Foale. He was chaired to his house after the declaration.

An even more interesting political first came three weeks later on 9 November, when the Town Council elected a lady mayor for the first time and, it was said, she was the first in Devon. Mrs Phillips was unanimously elected by the Town Council and had 'the whole-hearted support of the burgesses generally.' In proposing Mrs Phillips, Mr S.W. Hook, the retiring mayor, said 'The women of England had done work of great magnitude during the war and the country would have been the poorer had they not attempted what they had done.' Mrs Phillips was the wife of Mr T. Phillips of the firm of solicitors Every & Phillips, and had been engaged in the Effects Department of the War Office during the war. Although it was not mentioned in the local press at the time, she would have had a quiet (and hidden) smile on her face when she performed her first duty as mayor – that of welcoming Mr Hook to her first meeting as mayor – as she was a keen supporter of the Votes for Women movement. She could hardly have known at the time that she would go on to serve Honiton as its mayor for no less than 11 terms.

During the First World War a 13-year-old Honiton boy left the King Street National School to become a grocer's errand boy, and ended up owning the shop and being one of the most respected of Honiton's many worthy shopkeepers. Tom Bambury began that career working for three shillings and sixpence (17.5p) a week for Mr W.H. Foale whose High Street shop was opposite St Paul's Church. For that princely sum he had to work from 8a.m. until 8p.m. and, on Saturdays, until 10p.m. Unlike a later generation of errand boys who had bicycles, Tom delivered the groceries with a wheelbarrow as far as Tower Cross, a good and steep uphill mile, and to Major Weldon's at Tracey and all around Combe Raleigh.

Some 50 years later he recalled that the Christmas rush began six weeks before Christmas Day and the staff worked until 11p.m. weighing up the dates, biscuits, sugar and other delicacies. On his first Christmas Eve the shop stayed open until 11p.m. and then Tom was given his last delivery (to Mrs Pulman at Cowley) and finished work at 12.15 on Christmas morning.

At the time there were many special Christmas lines. Stockings with sweets ranged from three pence (just over $1^{1}/_{4}$p) to a shilling (5p), crackers from $4^{1}/_{2}$d ($3^{3}/_{4}$p) to half a crown (12 $^{1}/_{2}$p) for a four-foot long cracker that was packed with everything. Despite the war there were oranges at 15 for a shilling.

After a year Tom got a rise of sixpence a week ($2^{1}/_{2}$p) and was then invited to serve behind the counter. After three years he was earning 16 shillings (80p) and in 1922, when he was still only 20 years old,

Tom Bambury, the popular High Street grocer, pictured here during the Christmas rush in 1965. He is in his well-stocked shop.

he became the manager for Mr Foale (who died in 1922) and then for Mrs Foale until her death in 1936. The shop was then sold and he took over half of the premises, the other half becoming a butcher's shop. By 1932 he was earning £3.10.0d. (£3.50) a week.

It was not just at Christmas that shops were 'open all hours'. Honiton Fair was a great event for the grocery trade 75 years ago, when High Street was lined with stalls, many of them selling sweets supplied by Foale's – the staff weighed out a ton of almonds, cinnamons and comfits for the fair. Five or six times an evening Tom Bambury would wheel his barrow down to the Fair Field or along High Street, often to Mr Hill's sweet and hoopla stall which was one of the most popular that visited the town.

At the start of 1920 cinema goers at Honiton were able to watch a 'spectacular Picturisation (sic) of the World's great fairy story – Jack and the Bean Stalk.' The film was nearly 10,000 feet long and the cast included 1,300 children and real giants too – they included the tallest man in the world who was 8ft 6in tall. Honitonians, who saw the film either on the Monday or the Saturday performances at 3p.m. or 7p.m., talked about it for weeks afterwards.

Britain may not have become 'a Land Fit for Heroes' as the politicians had promised it would when the war was over, but Honiton's Town Council was doing its best, especially in the field of council housing of which there was a great shortage in the town. In February 1921 the town clerk told councillors that the Ministry of Health had sanctioned a loan of £22,220 to carry out their housing schemes. The tender of Messrs Chown & Son for the erection of six parlour-type houses at Dowell Street at £5,082.2s.4d. (£943.7s.0d.) each was accepted. An Exeter firm, Fothergill Bros, made the necessary roads and lay the sewers. Financial shortages delayed the work for some time.

George V died on 20 January 1936 at Sandringham and the nation was plunged into grief. At Honiton's St Michael's Church the bell was tolled during the morning and that of the parish church of St Paul's was tolled at noon. Both churches flew the Union Flag at half-mast. The mayor, Mr E.H. Brock, sent a message of sympathy on behalf of the town to Queen Mary:

Honiton, an old Borough, deeply regrets the death of the King. The loss will be keenly felt by everyone in the Borough. Honiton has always looked upon the King as being a great example to the Nation.

The Queen's private secretary replied: 'I am desired to convey to the Aldermen and Burgesses of Honiton the Queen's sincere thanks for your kind expression of sympathy in her irreparable loss.'

That evening a congregation of 300 attended a divine service of intercession by the rector, Revd A.A. Fane de Salis, at St Paul's Church.

Sleet, that later turned to snow, was falling on Wednesday when the mayor, Mr E.H. Brock, read the Proclamation of Edward VIII's accession shortly after noon from the balcony of the Market House. Despite the weather a crowd of several hundred was present including the Allhallows Officers' Training Corps in uniform and with fixed bayonets. A parade headed by the Town Band with draped drums marched to the church. It included the Honiton Platoon of the 4th Devons, the civic party and just about every body and organisation in the town, including the postmaster and his staff. After the service muffled bells were rung intermittently throughout the afternoon.

In February 1936 the Freedom of the Borough was conferred on Cyril Neville Tweed for his outstanding services to the town. They included that of being deputy town clerk from 1902–05; council member 1908–28; alderman of the borough 1922–28; mayor of the borough in 1908–09, 1909–10, 1916–17 and 1917–18; town clerk from 1926–32; and again as mayor in 1934–35. He was also the deputy coroner of East Devon and was the coroner in 1921. Among his non-civic interests was that of Honiton CC, of which he was president, and the Honiton Show for which he served as a committee member. As a former pupil of Allhallows School he served the Honitonian Club as secretary, started the first Scout troop in the town, was a vice-president of the YMCA and was the president of both Honiton Working Men's Club and the Honiton Swimming Club. He was the first of six people to receive the freedom of the town.

With his deep interest in the Boy Scout movement, Mr Tweed was among those who applauded the action later that year of Mr F. Cottrell of Marwood House who donated his property in Dowell Street (known as the Drill Hall) to the local troop for their headquarters. The Scouts had been using the building for about a year prior to the generous offer. Mr Cottrell's son officially handed over the building on 3 December 1936 because his father was ill. Among those present were Colonel A.D. Ackland, the county commissioner, and Sir Edward Cave, district commissioner, and Scoutmaster F. M. Lane. After the Wolf Cubs had given their Grand Howl, Mr Tucker showed lantern slides of Honiton Scout camps from 1924 onwards, which were said to be 'most interesting'. They would be even more so today. In its early days the premises of the Drill Hall had been used as a school – it became the Drill Hall later and was then used by the unemployed men of the town as a training centre. Around the time of the First World War the Scouts had their headquarters in New Street where the Scoutmaster was Roy Read, who founded Read's Garage. Lord Baden Powell started the Boy Scout Movement in 1908 and Honiton's troop was among the earliest in the country.

Honiton has always had a reputation for celebrating the high days in style, but the townsfolk excelled themselves on 12 May 1937 during the celebrations for the coronation of George VI. It was reported in *Pulman's Weekly News* as follows:

Never before have the townspeople of Honiton displayed such enthusiasm as at the Coronation Day celebrations. Throughout the week the wide High Street had worn a colourful dress of red, white and blue and was one of the gayest of pictures to motorists on the London to Exeter main road.

The pealing of the bells at St Michael's ushered in the day and that was followed by the civic parade that, after assembling at Bramble Hill, marched to St Paul's for a service of thanksgiving.

The Honiton Platoon of the 4th Devonshire Regiment headed the parade and was immediately followed by the mayor, Mrs J.M. Phillips, the town crier, John Lake, and the Corporation. Then every body and organisation in the town except one, from the Women's Institute to Cage Bird Society followed. The odd one out was the 1st Honiton Scout Troop who, under Scoutmaster F.M. Lane, were responsible for selling the souvenir programmes – something that the Scout movement had undertaken throughout the country.

St Michael's was packed with several hundred people outside following the proceedings via loudspeakers. The rector, Revd A.A. Fane de Salis, was supported by the Congregational minister, Revd G. Fellows, and the Methodist minister, Pastor W.T. Ashby. After the service the parade re-formed and marched to the Allhallows Playing Fields where it dispersed.

At noon over 700 children up to the age of 16 (including a day-old baby) received commemorative mugs and medals. The medals were the gift of the mayor who handed them to the children herself, the mugs being presented by the deputy mayor, Mr E.H. Brock. It was a busy day for the mayor who later handed out the prizes after the 30-event sports programme.

The civic party heads the parade making its way to St Paul's Church for the memorial service for Edward VII on 20 May 1910.

Above: *The church parade before the start of Honiton's celebrations for the coronation of George V in 1911.*

Below: *New Street, c.1912.*

Left: *The presentation of medals and mugs during Honiton's celebrations for the coronation of King George V in 1911, with the 1st Honiton Scout Troop forming a guard of honour.*

Honiton Rational Hospital Collectors, c.1912. These people collected money for the hospital.

The dedication of the 1st Honiton Scout Troop's flag at Sudbury Lawn in 1935. Although it was formed in 1910, two years after Lord Baden-Powell started the Boy Scout movement, the Honiton troop was not registered until 1922. They first met in King Street opposite the entrance to Streamers Meadows – since 1935 they have met at their Dowell Street HQ.

This page: *Scenes from George V's silver jubilee celebrations in Honiton in 1935 including the building of the giant bonfire that was built on the outskirts of the town.*

Above left and right: *Mourners file into St Paul's Church for the memorial service for George V in 1936.*

Left: *New Street residents preparing to celebrate the coronation of George VI in 1937.*

The 1st Honiton Boy Scout Troop in 1937. Left to right, back row: R. Boyland, R. Chivers, S. Goddard, F. Hill, B. Manley, B. Holiday, C. Holiday, C. Labdon, L. Moor; third row: P. Stuart, ?, J. Real (Rover Scout), W. Summers and H. Gregory (both patrol leaders), C. Davis (group leader), ?, J. Loverage (Rover Scout), ?, H. Long; second row: J. Prewer, E. Marks, F. Loverage and C. Greenslade (both Rover Scouts), Mr F. Lane (Scoutmaster), Mr Napier (president), W. Parker and N. Adette (both Rover Scouts), T. Salter, J. Warren; front row: W. Goddard, ? Manley, A. Lane, ?, ? Sansom, E. Prewer, ?, E. Tratt, R. Mutters, B. Bowen, J. Manley, ? Howard, 'Curly' Manley.

Later that day close on 2,500 burgesses sat down to a public tea in three large marquees, after which there was maypole and ballet dancing, a 'Pageant of Empire' by the pupils of the Honiton Junior School and a drill display by the girls of Honiton Senior School.

In the evening High Street was packed for outdoor dancing and 'although the traffic on the main London to Exeter road was light... police had very little difficulty in regulating the vehicles so as not to hamper the dancers.' Besides the outdoor dancing around 300 people, including the mayor and the rector, attended a dance at the Dolphin. A tired but happy town rounded off their day watching a 20-foot-high bonfire in the yard of Messrs Kirton. In an age when floodlit church towers are anything but a novelty, it might be of interest to learn that:

... great surprise was shown at the manner in which St Michael's was illuminated with red flares by Mr R. Tucker who had done the same on the occasion of Queen Victoria's Golden Jubilee in 1887 and the Silver Jubilee of King George V and Queen Mary in 1936.

The next day Honiton obtained its permanent memorial of the great day when the mayor accepted the 'Glen' on behalf of the people of the town. Major H.H. Lilley handed over the part of the wooded glade which was in his possession and had been improved by townspeople's donations and subscriptions.

Last but not least, the inmates at the workhouse each received a shilling (5p) from the Public Assistance Committee. They also had tea and were given cigarettes.

Unlike the First World War, the Second World War came as no surprise, most Britons having been resigned to the fact that Germany would have to be dealt with for well over a year. The news of the First World War had burst on a largely unsuspecting nation that had enjoyed a sunny August bank holiday a day or so before. During 1938 and '39 fears that war was just around the corner affected even such peaceable bodies as the Boy Scouts at Honiton, who received courses in air-raid precautions, and there was an increase in the number of scouts taking the Fireman's Badge.

Unlike 1914, in 1939 there was the fear that cities could be badly damaged by air attacks and children and some mothers were evacuated to the country-side. East Devon was an obvious choice because of its lack of large towns or cities and heavy industry. Honiton was chosen as the detraining centre for a wide area that included Honiton Borough Council, Honiton Rural District Council, Sidmouth Urban Council and Ottery St Mary Urban District Council.

The children began arriving during the evening of Friday 1 September, the day the German army invaded Poland. An advance guard of 300 children from Peckham was billeted in the town after being fed

in the Mackarness Hall. Within three days nearly 3,000 children had found homes in the area. Nurses and ambulances were waiting at the station to deal with any casualties but happily they were not needed. All the children received a meal and rations at the schools, where they were grouped for conveyance to the districts and their new homes. Arrangements at the station were in the hands of Major A.L. Harrison of Farway, who had the assistance of council officials and the stationmaster, Mr S. Towler, and his staff.

It was reported in *Pulman's Weekly News* that 'members of the teaching staffs who came with the children were warm in their praise of the arrangements which had been made' and paid striking tributes to the women of the town, headed by the mayor (Mrs J.M. Phillips), who did everything in their power to make the children comfortable. It also said that 'the spirit of the children was remarkable... they have settled down happily... they were seeing rabbits and cows for the first time.' Obviously that worthy paper was toeing the official line in the manner of its report-ing, but however poverty-stricken their lives and homes in the East End of London might have been, the children were torn from their families and sent on a 150-mile train journey into the unknown. I was only eight when I went with my mother to 'choose' an evacuee at Seaton Town Hall and I will never forget the weeping and wailing.

Pulman's Weekly News itself had already placed itself on a war footing; the 16 pages of eight columns each had quickly been changed into an eight-page and seven-column paper. Most daily papers quickly shrunk, most being down to only four pages when the war ended.

By the evening of 3 September Honiton borough had 239 new inhabitants with a further 194 expected, Ottery St Mary had 334, Sidmouth had 375 and another 315 were expected. In the Honiton Rural District Council area the numbers were: Branscombe 28, Awliscombe 70, Gittisham 58, Luppitt 87, Broadhembury 92, Yarcombe 37, Buckerell 34, Talaton 65, Upottery 65, Payhembury 35, Sheldon 32, Dunkeswell 40, Combe Raleigh 22, Monkton 35, Wilmington 21, Offwell 35, Cotleigh Farway 45, Northleigh 32 and Plymtree 31.

The town's Air Raid Precautions (ARP) personnel were quickly brought up to wartime strength and its Auxillary Fire Service (AFS) was on duty day and night – it had been allocated a trailer pump. The Allhallows Chapel was adapted as a First Aid Post and the infants centre was used for demonstrations on how to fit children's gas masks. The headquarters of the Honiton Police Division in High Street became the communications centre in case of an air attack and was protected by 3,000 sandbags.

Complaints about lights showing during the blackout were to become commonplace – the first local man to be fined for such an offence was Albert

The inspection of Honiton Home Guard by the mayor, A.F. Studley, on 16 May 1943.

Honiton Civil Defence Force receives delivery of a new rescue wagon during the Second World War (1942). The mayor, A.F. Studley, is fifth from the left.

Edward Jenkins, a haulage contractor from Broadhembury who was fined ten shillings (50p) by the Honiton magistrates for not having the correct shields on the headlights of his car. Authority did tend to be paranoid in times of war and anyone seen lighting a cigarette was quickly told by an air-raid warden or policemen to 'put that light out'. The chances of a German pilot being able to see a lit match or a glowing cigarette, from 2,000 or 3,000 feet was nil.

On the civic front there no change, Mrs J.M. Phillips was appointed mayor for the ninth time, a remarkable tribute to a woman who was, according to the 'father' of the Chamber, Alderman W.H. Barnes, 'a striking example to those people in the town who stayed outside the Council and did nothing but criticise.' Mr E.H. Brook was also reappointed as deputy mayor.

In the immediate aftermath of Dunkirk, when the threat of invasion was real, the War Minister, Anthony Eden, appealed on the radio for volunteers to form the LDV (Local Defence Volunteers), quickly renamed the Home Guard and immortalised as Dad's Army in the TV comedy series of that name.

Honiton's Home Guard paraded at the Allhallows Playing Fields until its stand down on 31 December 1944 when the danger of invasion was long past. They guarded vital places such as railway bridges, and factories, and in 1944 provided England's defence during the D-Day preparations. Honiton's Home Guard, along with the Offwell Home Guard and the US Troops at Heathfield Army Camp, guarded Honiton Tunnel. That duty involved a platoon, complete with telephonists, runners and a first-aid party, entrenched at either end with double lines of field telephone laid to connect with the Platoon HQ. These duties were carried out between 24 April and 10 July and involved a total of 11,000 attendances.

Soon after the outbreak of the Second World War an army camp was built on the western outskirts of the town. Among the regiments to be stationed there were the Devons, the Royal Ulster Rifles, No. 2 Training Bn. REME, the Durham Light Infantry, the Wessex Brigade (consisting of the Devon and Dorset Regiment, the Gloucester Regiment, the Royal Hampshire Regiment and the Duke of Edinburgh's Royal Regiment), the ATS and, during the countdown to the Normandy landings on D-Day, American troops. The camp also housed Italian POWs for a spell and it is claimed, almost certainly incorrectly, that Barnes Wallis built the prototype of his 'Dams' bomb there.

After the Second World War the REME entered a team in the Exeter and District (now Devon and Exeter) Football League with some success, the Senior I titles being won in 1951–52 and in 1958–59. However, the inability to play at fixture on a scheduled day due to military commitments led to the team being fined, and they withdrew from the league.

By the late 1950s military spending was cut and one of the early casualties was to be Heathfield Army Camp. The forthcoming closure of the camp made the headlines in the *News Of The World* in 1959 and, given that newspaper's track record, it comes as no surprise to learn that it was the romantic side of the closure that had attracted them. 'There Will Be Broken Hearts When The Troops Leave Town' was the headline and the article claimed that there would be 100 lonely girls in the little market town of Honiton in four short months. They were the sweethearts of the men of No. 2 Training Bn. REME who were leaving the town in April. And it was not just the girls who would be missing out – the local shops and inns would lose quite a lot of trade, especially the Vine Inn whose landlady, Irene Manley, said that:

... it will make a big difference to our trade... we have a rock and roll room, which is packed most nights. It has a £1,000 juke box they can dance to and many a girl has met her future husband there.

According to the *News of the World* a cynic said 'The local chaps will have to stop drinking cider and start taking girls out instead.'

Two views of Heathfield Army Camp, one shows the Guard Room in the 1960s (left), the other is around 1972. It is obvious that the military have left; no sergeant major would have the hut surrounds in such a shocking state.

In fact there were still a small number of troops left because the camp was used as a staging-post for personnel in transit until at least 1962. What was certain was that almost overnight the population of the town fell by just over 1,000 people – and the rates rose by 40 per cent.

In the end the camp was offered to the East Devon District Council for £155,000. It was, they said, a snip – being converted into an industrial estate, as well as developed for housing, and its eventual proximity to the new A30 dual carriageway (which puts it within ten miles or 15 minutes of both Exeter Airport and the M5), meant that it certainly was. Mr Geoff Hulley, managing director of East Devon Small Industries Group, based at Heathpark, said in 1998 that Honiton was 'destined soon to be the most industrialised of the seven major towns in East Devon.'

In 1972 the camp was used to accommodate the Ugandan Asians and was a resettlement centre for them. At first there were said to be 1,600 unfortunate people fleeing from the villainous dictator Idi Amin and heading for Honiton; in the event around 1,200 turned up.

There was a lot of adverse comment about the squalid conditions at Heathfield, but not from the Uganda Asians who were full of praise for the help they received and the friendliness shown by the people of the town. But there was criticism from the press – so much so that local MP Mr (later Sir) Peter Emery made a visit and found nothing to justify the criticism. The town clerk also issued a statement pointing out that the situation had developed out of one person writing an unsupported letter after making a fleeting visit.

When the district council placed the homeless in the huts, it was not an ideal solution and led to many complaints about dangerous floors, rats, broken windows and ice-cold conditions in winter. Like the wheels of justice, those of district councils move exceedingly slow, but by the end of the twentieth century both the camp and the homeless were just memories for a steadily decreasing number of people.

During the building of an extension to the industrial park in 1992 wartime shells and mortar bombs were uncovered and, after the bomb-disposal squad was called in for a second time, the work was halted until the entire site had been subjected to a clean

The end of an era. Roger Olds of the demolition firm B. Olds of Exmouth working on the demolition of the last buildings at the old Heathfield Army Camp in 1993.

Ugandan Asian refugees walking in High Street at the time they were billeted at the old Heathfield Army camp in 1972.

Distribution of Food Gifts from the Tanganyika Food for Britain Fund at Dar-es-Salaam to the 12 inhabitants at the St Margaret's Almshouses on 31 March 1949 by the deputy mayor, Alderman A.F.Studley. He is presenting a tin of beef dripping to Mr Vanstone while the other recipients wait their turn. Today the aid goes in the opposite direction.

sweep. They discovered and made safe several more items during the search, but the delays led to an extra £8,740 being added to the contract price.

Before all that happened signs that the Second World War was ending began on 31 December 1944, when the Home Guard held its last parade to mark their official standing down. The week before VE Day (8 May 1945), however, Honiton Town Council were told by he Regional War Commission that they did not have permission to demolish the air-raid shelter outside Lloyds Bank because the Minister of Transport did not consider it to be a danger to the public.

No amount of petty officialdom was going to interfere a week later when Honiton joyfully celebrated the official end of the war in Europe. There was no official celebration, Honitonians taking it on themselves to celebrate – especially in Littletown where the road was covered from end to end by tables groaning under the weight of cakes and sandwiches. In the middle of Littletown Road an enormous bonfire was lit and kept going for 48 hours by women who, 'being helped in their spring cleaning, continually added articles of furniture of considerable antiquity'. Blazing tar barrels were also rolled in the street.

Singing and dancing in the street went on until midnight on VE Day and VE Day Plus One; Mr W. Broomfield led the festivities with Mr J. Chester accompanying him on the piano accordion. In all 183 Littletown children attended the tea party and were joined by 199 officers and men of a Royal Marines detachment that were shooting at the local firing range. Children's sports were held in one of Frank Walden's fields.

There were other parties in the town, including ones at Queen Street and Dowell Street and, like every bonfire lit that night, there were effigies of Hitler and Mussolini on both. A dance was held in the fire station and those adults at the Public Assistance

Institute (the new name for the workhouse) were not forgotten, a meat tea being provided.

All the celebrations were muted by the thought that the war against Japan was still going on, as was underlined when the news reached the town of the death in action of Honitonian Private Harold John Franks. He had been killed by small-arms fire in Burma in April, and he was buried at Mimnui near Mandalay but, oddly enough, his name does not appear on the town's war memorial outside St Paul's Church, which suggests that he had left the town and is recorded on a war memorial elsewhere.

VJ Day (Victory over Japan) on 15 August 1945 saw the end of the Second World War and, like VE Day some three months earlier, was the cause of great rejoicing nationwide. In Honiton between 700 and 800 members of the ATS, accompanied by their drums, marched to St Paul's Church for a service of thanksgiving that was followed by sports in the afternoon in the Allhallows Playing Fields. Again Littletown held its own celebrations with 200 children having tea with 300 people enjoying supper that evening before a huge bonfire was lit and fireworks were followed by singing and dancing 'until a very late hour'.

In July the result of the first general election for ten years was announced. Voting in Honiton and the rest of the country took place on 5 July but, in order to allow time for the postal votes of the armed forces to arrive, the results were not announced until 26 July. Even then there were still 13 constituencies still to declare.

The result was a landside victory for Labour, giving them their first ever majority government with an overall majority of 146. No less than 13 Conservative ministers lost their seats. The Honiton constituency had been a Conservative seat ever since it was formed when the town of Honiton had been disenfranchised in 1868, and it stayed that way in 1945 despite a drop in Mr (later Sir) Cedric Drewe's majority – although the increased electorate meant that the number of votes cast for him had been increased by just over 1,500. Honiton was one of the safer seats in the country and the final results that were announced from the balcony of the Dolphin Hotel were:

Mr Cedric Drewe (Conservative)	*24,499*
Mr R.T. Langdon (Labour)	*12,739*
Majority	*11,760*

In the 1935 general election the result had been:

Mr Cedric Drewe (Conservative)	*22,805*
Mr J. Morris (Labour)	*8,916*
Majority	*13,889*

Mr Drewe's agent, Captain Jeffrey Gibbs, was continuing a remarkable political family record. Captain

Gibbs's father was the agent for the Honiton division before him and his grandfather, Joseph Gibbs, was agent for the Newport, Monmouth, constituency – between them the three men never lost an election.

Another change that peace brought was the lowering of the 'Stars and Stripes' at the nearby Dunkeswell airfield on 31 July. That flag had first been raised on the hilltop air base in September 1943 when it became the main US Naval Air Base in the United Kingdom. It was from here that Fleet Air Wing 7 functioned to support surface craft in the anti-submarine warfare in the Atlantic Ocean and the Bay of Biscay, flying Consolidated Liberators (B29) and Consolidated Catalina aircraft. The 183 officers and men who were killed on active service on operations from Dunkeswell, or died later of wounds, are remembered on a plaque just inside the south door of the St Nicholas's Church. Among them is Joseph Kennedy, son of the wartime American Ambassador to the United Kingdom who reported back to President Roosevelt that England was finished after Dunkirk. Joe Kennedy's brother, John, would later become the American president.

Joe Kennedy and another officer actually died on a very special mission from an East Anglian aerodrome, but Dunkeswell was his home base. When the Americans left, RAF Transport Command moved in.

The organ at St Nicholas's Church was a gift from the American Navy in 1965 and two extra stops were given later.

That autumn the British Restaurant in the Pannier Market was closed. The mayor and mayoress, Alderman F. and Mrs E.M. Studley, had opened it on 2 May 1943 and its purpose was to provide hot meals outside of rationing restrictions at reasonable prices. A cooked dinner cost a shilling (5p) and, although I cannot speak from experience as far as Honiton's British Restaurant was concerned, I was often taken by my grandmother to the one at Sidmouth. Despite being of tender years at the time, I can well remember the delicious dinners served there.

Honiton's restaurant had hardly broken even in the last six months of the war and the Ministry of Food sanctioned its closure when the Town Council indicated that it was not interested in running it. The mayor, Clifford Hatcher, paid tribute to the cook supervisor, Mrs Mulpeter, and her voluntary staff. He said, 'It is invidious to mention names but, besides Mrs Mulpeter, two stand out – Mrs Morton Moncrief and Mrs Stanley.'

In Victorian times and until the outbreak of the First World War in 1914 Honiton's ceremonial occasions turned to Honiton Volunteer Band for their music. The outbreak of war ended the band for the duration and, in the 1920s, it was mainly the work and driving force of Ernest Connett and six of his sons, who all played, that restarted the band. They were

Bernard, Charles, Claude, Don, Ernest (junr) and Ralph, and their playing led to the formation of a Town Borough Band, or the Honiton Silver Prize Band. They had the benefit of a musical father, Ernest Arthur Connett, a shoemaker and a former sergeant major who was the bandmaster of the F (Honiton) Company, Devon Regiment before the First World War. He bought a piano and before very long the family was appearing at local dance halls, billed as 'The Connetts Dance Band'.

Only those who have served on an organisation's committee can really appreciate the amount of work that goes on behind the scenes in order to present a seemingly smooth-running event to the outsider. Honiton Silver Prize Band was no exception. Happily the minute book for the years 1935–39 are still in existence. They make fascinating reading and show only too well just what organisation and work, and sometimes minutiae, are needed to provide the finished product – a band playing at a local fête or on a summer's evening at the nearby seaside town.

One such cause for the backroom activity in 1935 was the production of a concert in aid of the new instrument fund. Among the instruments needed were a soprano and a tenor cornet, although in the case of the former negotiations were underway with the Ottery St Mary Band who had one to spare. Two practices a night were required and the cost of hiring the YMCA was partially met by the bandsmen, who paid two pence an evening (boys paid a penny).

Some 50 posters were produced and an advert was placed in the *East Devon County Press* although, in the end, the secretary, Donald Connett, managed to get it accepted as a news item. Then there were 200 programmes printed and sold at two pence each – the printing, by Mr Dimond, cost 12s.6d. The WI wanted 10s. for the hire of their piano, although it was reduced to 5s. after the first night, and they also asked for 10s. for the use of the curtain. The band did not need the curtain and asked for a reduction in the cost of hiring the piano, on the grounds that they only needed about six songs to be accompanied. The WI also had 72 chairs on offer at a penny each; these, along with 150 hired from Mr Real (also at a penny each), plus those already in the Drill Hall, meant that there would be seating for about 290 people. Council office mandarins were more relaxed about crowded halls in those days. There does not appear to be an outcome of the concert's silver collection in the minute book.

The main source of income for the band was their charge for playing at fêtes, flower shows and carnivals throughout East Devon, where they were always a welcome feature. These charges were usually in the region of £7.10s.0d. (£7.50) to £10, and even up to £16 for an all-day engagement. That may not seem much in today's money but, at first blush, those charges struck me as being rather high for the 1930s when a farmworker was lucky if he took home two

Above: *The Honiton Volunteer Band in 1900.*

Below and right: *An unknown royal occasion.*

The military and Honiton Town Band march down High Street on, judging by the bunting and flags, a coronation or jubilee between the two world wars.

The mayor and mayoress, Mr and Mrs A.F. Studley, tuck in after the opening ceremony of the British Restaurant on 2 May 1943. The town clerk, Mr Coates, is on the left and the mayor's chaplain, Mr J.E.L. Logan is in front. Among those queuing to be served are Mr Hatcher, Mr Turner and Mr Davey.

pounds a week. But of course seven to ten pounds had to pay for around 20 bandsmen, the capital outlay for instruments and uniforms and the hire of a charabanc to take them to the engagement. The hirers were expected to supply tea for the band and, for all-day engagements, sometimes lunch as well.

The organisations hiring them were as eager as the band in cutting costs and frequently asked for a reduction – some succeeded but not very often as Honiton Silver Prize Band lived in a competitive world and could not afford to overcharge. But they did have overheads and the members gave up many hours during the week to provide excellent entertainment. Such were their standards that, without a doubt, whoever was engaging them was getting the best band in the neighbourhood.

The celebrations to mark George V's silver jubilee offer one such example. Charles Connett, the band chairman, told his committee that the question of the band had been brought up at the last Jubilee Committee meeting and that the chairman had said that the band would get ten pounds for the day. Mr Connett said that ten pounds would not be enough, but the mayor, who was present, told him that 'the band was practically honour-bound to do the civic part of the ceremony (9a.m. to midday).' The Honiton Silver Prize Band, armed with the knowledge that the Exmouth Band was getting £25 for the day, decided to ask for £16.

When 1939 began, with the countdown to 3 September, the band was accepting more and more engagements for the opening part of 1940 that, in the event, never took place. In June, bandsmen of the appropriate age signed 'army papers' and a week later a committee meeting was held to pick NCOs for the Territorial Band. Britain was at war on 3 September and 20 bandsmen became the Band of the 5th Devons

who went on to play at concerts and parades all over Britain, before being demobilised in 1945 or 1946.

The future of the band was raised at a Town Council meeting in November 1945 but nothing was agreed, because 'few members of the of the original band were back in the town.' The re-formation waited until 1956, when the chance discovery of the Honiton Silver Prize Band's instruments (in a loft above the Town Council's offices, then in Sudbury Lawn in High Street) by the town clerk, Harry Vernon, led to the forming of the Royal British Legion Brass Band. Harry Vernon contacted the mayor, Alderman J.R. Board, who approached Jim Kendall with the suggestion of forming a band. Jim protested that although he ran a dance band he did not have a clue about brass bands. The mayor pulled rank and Honiton again had a band.

The Connetts, especially Donald, who was bandmaster in 1958, played a big part in restarting the band. At first there were 'hundreds of volunteers' who wanted to become members, but when they realised the work involved and the need to learn how to play an instrument, many of them fell by the wayside. Over the years numbers have fluctuated, but at the time of writing (2004) there are 27 members – and new members are always welcome. Like the pre-war band, the brass band has become part of Honiton's passing days – probably more so than any other organisation in the town. Carnivals, fêtes, flower shows – you name it they are there and they have played at almost every town and village in East Devon and beyond. They even played in France on 29 May 2003, when around 20 members went with the official party to mark the 30th anniversary of twinning links with Mézidon-Canon; on that day they played on four occasions and in three different halls. On one of the occasions they played with their Mézidon-Canon opposite numbers, the Fanfare de Mézidon-Canon. It goes without saying, however, that their most important engagement is on Remembrance Sunday.

The 'craze' of twinning by English towns and villages, mostly with French towns and villages with similar industrial or environmental backgrounds, was sweeping the country by the 1970s. Honiton joined the craze following a public meeting on 4 September 1972, when it was formally resolved to enter into twinning arrangements with Mézidon-Canon, a small town south-east of Caen just off the main N13 road to Lisieux and, eventually, Paris. Its main attractions are the castle and the abbey.

The charter was first signed in France in 1973 and the French party visited Honiton in the following year, when the charter received the seal of the borough that was affixed by the town clerk, Albert Johnson. It was one of the last occasions on which the seal was officially used – it was phased out by the local government changes. The seal was not placed on the charter in 1973 at Mézidon-Canon as it is not allowed to leave the borough. The mayor of

The Burgomaster of Gronau, Herr Horst Witchman, with Honiton's mayor, Walt Summers, pictured at the twinning ceremony between the town towns on 19 September 1987. Honiton's town clerk, Ivor Biddington, is on the left.

Mézidon-Canon, M. Henry Delisle, and his three deputies led the French party.

In September 1987 Honiton twinned again, this time with the German town of Gronau, near the border of the old East Germany, and Honitonians have looked at the East German guards through binoculars as they patrolled the border wire fence. The schools of both towns established the first links. Gronau is also twinned with Mézidon-Canon. Twinning has not been without its upsets. In 1998 some councillors said that the 700th anniversary celebrations of Gronau should come before Honiton's fair and hot pennies ceremony – in so doing so they incurred the wrath of the mayor, Mrs Joanna Bull.

Only illness should prevent the Mayor attending the fair ceremony... I am not prepared to see an ancient tradition cast aside... the fair was one of those traditional civic occasions when the Mayor is dressed in full regalia... to sweep it aside spelled the beginning of the end for such traditions.

In 2001, at a special meeting of the Honiton Twinning Association, former chairman Gill Nicholls said that:

... although the Committee had actively pursued twinning with many exchanges, the responsibility for organization had fallen on just four or five members and, unfortunately, there appeared little or no interest from the Honiton community.

A long-felt need in Honiton finally reached fruition towards the end of the century when, in September 1998, the Heathpark Community Project was opened. The press handout said that:

... the dreams of parents and children of Heathpark have finally come true. Hopefully we will no longer see the headlines 'parents anger over teeny terrors or, parents fight to save playground'.

East Devon District Council, through joint funding arrangements with the Devon and Cornwall Housing Association, and the Sovereign Housing Association

Above: *Timothy, Daniel and Jaime Herrett in the damp bedroom they shared at the Heathpark site in 1982.*

Right: *Vanessa and Angela Eyres pictured with their children outside the huts on the Heathpark site.*

(all of whom own properties on the estate), together with the support of the Devon Playing Fields Association, have achieved the completion of the children's play area. East Devon District Council provided a flat on the estate for a development worker who introduced such activities as a youth club, first aid, play schemes, arts and crafts, and cooking evenings, and older members have taken part in debating drug education. The flat provides a tuck shop, TV and video, snooker table, CD player and also a washing machine and tumble dryer. The result has been a definite reduction in the number of complaints of anti-social behaviour.

Honiton entered the third millennium a vibrant and forward-looking community. The arrival of the Tesco supermarket obviously had some affect on the town's High Street shops, but neither Tesco nor any other large shopping chain can match the high standards, both in service and in quality, that can be found in High Street and New Street, and the town continues to attract people both to shop and live.

However, not everything in the town was thriving in the early years of the twenty-first century. Honiton Horticultural Society was wound up in 2004 after being a welcome part of the town's social life for 77 years. Falling numbers in membership led to this decision and the society held its last meeting on 21 July in the Mackarness Hall, where its funds were donated to local charities. Where possible the society's trophies were returned to their original donors or their surviving relations and others were lodged with the Allhallows Museum.

Gender equality is obviously very important. Since 1997 the MP for the Tiverton and Honiton constituency has been Angela Browning – in May 2001 Revd Canon Jane Hedges became Honiton's team rector – the first lady in a long list of Honiton rectors – and in 2001 and 2002 Ruth Robson was

elected as mayor. For the first time in its long and remarkable history Honiton had ladies as its monarch, member of parliament, rector and mayor.

Jane Hedges was ordained deaconess in June 1980 and served in the parish of Holy Trinity with St Columba Fareham in the Portsmouth Diocese. Three years later she moved to the Southampton city centre team ministry where she served as a team vicar. After being made a deacon in 1987 in Winchester Cathedral, she moved to Waterlooville the following year and served as diocesan stewardship adviser in the Portsmouth diocese. She was appointed as residentiary canon at Portsmouth Cathedral in 1993 where she served as canon pastor until 2001. She was priested in May 1994 along with 11 other women in the diocese of Portsmouth and moved to Honiton in May 2001 as team rector. She was married to Chris in 1982 and they have two sons, Jonathan (13) and Adam (11).

Angela Browning was unsuccessful in her first attempt to win a seat – she lost to Gwynneth Dunwoody in the Labour stronghold of Crewe and Nantwich in the 1987 general election, but was adopted for the Tiverton constituency and won the seat in 1992. She retained the seat in 1997, when changes to its boundary saw Honiton transferred and renamed the Tiverton and Honiton constituency. She retained the seat in 2001 and won again in 2005.

Although a Honitonian by parentage, the mayor at the time of writing, Sally Casson, was actually born at Salcombe Regis near Sidmouth in 1947, and was educated at the Mares Convent in Ottery St Mary. But, apart from ten years when her husband Roy was employed by Westlands at Yeovil and they moved to that town, she has spent all her life in Honiton. She joined the Town Council in 1999 and was elected mayor in 2004. Sally and Ronald have two daughters – Sarah and Rebecca.

An artist's impression of what the new Tesco store off Sidmouth Road would look like. He was not far out.

Local farmers protesting at Honiton's Tesco store in the 1990s over the vast difference in their profit on a lamb and that of the supermarket giant. They have a point.

Above and right: *The Old Honitonians' clubhouse and the School House and dining-hall at Allhallows School, c.1918.*

Below: *Allhallows Playing Field, c.1918.*

Above and left: *Of special interest is this view of the north side of the Allhallows Museum in the 1950s, which shows the smaller building to the left that, although belonging to the museum, was rented to the County Library. The view of the front door shows the phone box that once stood outside the museum.*

Chapter 5
Allhallows Chapel, School and Museum

All that remains today of the ancient medieval Allhallows Chapel is the small building next to St Paul's Church, now occupied by the Allhallows Museum. The original chapel certainly existed as far back as 1327 when it was mentioned in the cartulary (the register of the title deeds to the lands, liberties and privileges of the abbey) of Newenham Abbey at Axminster. On that occasion the reference was in connection with a dispute between John de Carew and the abbey.

Apparently it was never well maintained, according to Farquharson in his *History of Honiton* '... in 1418 it [the chapel] was out of repair and an indulgence of 40 days would be granted to all who contributed to its support.' Earlier, in 1406, a John Chepman left £10 'for the roofing of the Chapel of All Saints if the parishioners would cover it with lead.' He must have had a suspicion that they would not because he stipulated that if they would not do so his executors were 'to dispose of the money at their discretion'.

In 1429 the good people of Honiton petitioned the Pope that they:

... desired to have Mass celebrated daily at dawn by a fit priest at their own expense in the Chapel of All Saints, built with bell tower and bell within the bounds of the parish church of St Michael on account of the perils of the roads and on account of the floods of the waters which flow between the said church and town.

St Michael's, of course, sat on the hill overlooking the town, and it was a long walk to attend services there, especially for the elderly and infirm. It was closed in the mid-nineteenth century and was replaced with the present parish church of St Paul's.

There are many references to wealthy parishioners making bequests towards the upkeep of Allhallows Chapel including, in 1542, the founding of the Allhallows Charity by Sir John Kirkham, knight, and Eliseus Harding, clerk. The charity was to help keep the chapel in a state of good repair.

We know that the chapel consisted of a nave and a chancel joined together by a central tower, but by the start of the eighteenth century it was in a poor state of repair and was not used for services. In fact, in 1712 the tower and nave were pulled down and the site stood empty until 1743, when a new chapel was built. Some 22 years later the great fire of 1765 destroyed it. The chancel of the original building remained, however, and it was used as a

classroom of Allhallows School that had been founded in 1524 by Sir John Kirkham and Eliseus Harding. It was at first a charity school and part of the Allhallows Chapel until 1712, when it became a separate building. In 1835 the chapel was demolished to make room for St Paul's Church that was to replace St Michael's as the parish church. The schoolroom that had served as such for nearly two centuries was not touched and it became, in turn, the school's dining-room. In 1903 it was used as a school chapel to serve as a memorial of those Old Honitonians who had been killed in the Boer War (1899–1902).

A swimming-pool was built at the school in around 1912 but was later filled in. In 1913 Chris Turner, a builder whose premises were at West End, built the clubhouse for the Old Honitonians Club. It was said at the time that vandals burnt it down in around the 1970s.

Lack of space led to Allhallows School looking for new premises in the 1930s and, when plans to build a bigger school in Honiton itself fell through because of funding difficulties, Allhallows moved to Rousdon, 15 miles away on the Devon–Dorset border between Seaton and Lyme Regis, where it acquired the Rousdon Manor and estate of the Peek family. The handsome building, completed in 1878, had cost Sir Henry Peek £250,000 to build. No doubt, with an

Allhallows Museum.

Middlemist House, Allhallows School, Rugby XV, 1933–34.

Right: *Old Honitonians' Cricket Week in 1925. Left to right, back row: B.C. Hale, G.H.R. Dew, J.L. Felton, E.M. Smythe, J.W. Sandoe, E.H. Brock; front row: E.W. Byrde, H.W. Cobb, J. Ellison, F.C. Drake, E.C. Dolman.*

Middlemist House, Allhallows School, Rugby XV, 1937–38. Left to right, back row: F.A. Parsons, P.B. May, A.T.H. Glanvill (later Dr Terry Glanvill), G.J. Money, T. Whetstone, J.P. Osborne, N.S. Sherrard-Smith, G.E. May; middle row: P.E. Stumbles, M.A. Rice, P.H.E. Thomas, S.J. Harper, A.G. Sherrard-Smith; front row: D.F. Sear, R.D. Anderson. C.D. Wilson also played in the team but was absent on this occasion. Results: beat Baker House 56–0, beat Chudleigh House 48–10, beat Stanton House 12–0.

annual income of £5 million (roughly a pound a minute) he could afford it. But the shrewd business-man, who had made his money in groceries and the tea trade, would have turned in his grave if he had known that his home would be sold 60 years later for £25,000 – one tenth of what he had spent on it.

The school moved lock, stock and barrel at the end of the spring term in 1938, that had been ended two weeks early to allow sufficient time for the Brighton firm entrusted with the removal to finish the job. They were not entrusted with the Officers' Training Corps' armoury or the contents of the labo-ratories; members of the staff in their cars took them to Rousdon.

At the last Speech Day in Honiton (1937) the head-master, Mr G. Swallow, told parents that the school was practically full with 120 boarders and 20 day pupils. That year had seen the arrival of tennis as a recognised school game.

Allhallows School was at Rousdon for only a few more years than the Peek family. At the end of the twentieth century the school was closed because of financial problems and in 2004 the building is still in the process of being developed into flats and housing.

Probably the most famous Old Honitonian was Sir Arthur 'Bomber' Harris, leader of Bomber Command during much of the Second World War, including all the 1,000 bomber raids. He was a pupil at Allhallows School during the Edwardian era. Due to Churchill's decision to distance himself from the thousands of civilians killed and cities razed to the ground on his orders, and the Labour Government's attitudes, Harris was the only senior commander not to get a peerage. But the town of Honiton knew the immense debt the country owed him for his part in winning the war. He accepted the Honorary Freedom of the Borough on Tuesday 24 July 1945 – just days before the events at Hiroshima overshadowed even the destruction his 1,000 bomber raids had caused.

The mayor, Mr C.N. Hatcher, welcomed Sir Arthur in the Mackarness Hall, close to the old Allhallows School buildings, and said that he had been a great sportsman, gaining his school colours at rugby, cricket and hockey, and had been *Victor Ludorum* for one year. The local Air Training Corps provided a guard of honour, and it would be interesting to know how many of them joined the Royal Air Force and what the highest rank was that any of them reached.

After the move to Rousdon the school building was sold off and used during the Second World War as an ARP (Air Raid Precautions) first-aid post. In 1946 some local people who were worried that it might be demolished, purchased it for £2,000 and it was opened as a museum in November of that year as the Honiton and Allhallows Museum. It is listed as a Grade II building. It has, according to J.W.R. Coxhead, 'the original cast windows of the early fourteenth-century Chapel of Allhallows'. It was acquired originally to house the John Murch collec-tion of Honitonia. Mr Murch was on the original committee and was the last of a long line of Huguenot refugees from the Low Countries, the family being established in Honiton as clockmakers, and ironmongers. Among his collection was an old clock with a Murch dial and, less than a stone's throw from the museum, there is a clock made by Matthew Murch in 1851 in St Paul's tower.

The first curator was Mrs Esme Nicholl who held the position for many years. It was largely her efforts that put the embryonic museum on a sound financial footing. She was still serving on the committee in 1970. Thanks to her, following the discovery of pre-historic bones during excavations for the building of the Honiton bypass, enough were retained in Honiton to form a worthwhile display. The 100,000-year-old collection consists of fossilised bones of elephants, hippopotami, red deer and giant ox, and they are housed in a case just inside the door.

Honiton is known throughout the world for its former lace-manufacturing industry and it will come as no surprise to find probably the best collection in the world of Honiton and Continental lace from the sixteenth, seventeenth and eighteenth centuries on display at the museum.

In 1969 the fabric of the museum was in a very dangerous condition and urgent repairs were needed. Help in funding the work included grants from the Borough Council, Devon County Council and the Pilgrim Trust.

Overcrowding had long been a problem when, in 1995, the chance to purchase an adjoining cottage in Church Street was quickly taken up. The building cost £50,000, of which £15,000 had come from a purchase fund, the balance coming from grants from the East Devon District Council, Honiton Town Council, the Market Trust, the Esme Fairburn Trust, the Mercers Company and a private donor.

Rosemary Connett (left) *and a fellow lacemaker working on lace at Allhallows Museum in c.2000.*

Middlemist House, Allhallows School, Hockey XI, 1936–37. Left to right, back row: A.P. Stumbles, T. Whetstone, R.N. Heard, M.A. Rice, D.G. Emmerson, N.S. Sherrard-Smith; front row: A.G. Sherrard-Smith, P.E. Stumbles, R.J. Boret, P.G. Tyler, Y. Fitzgerald, D. Hamley, P.H.E. Thomas. Results: drew 3–3 with Walpole House, beat Balet House 2–0, beat Chudleigh House 2–0.

Allhallows Museum in 1990.

Chapter 6
Schools

Remembered by the late Edgar William Pulman, Margaret Robson and Keith Eddey

There follow the memories of Edgar William Pulman, recorded in 1989:

I started in the infants class in 1912 at the age of four; the class was located in the girls' section. One of my teachers was a Miss Voysey, a middle-aged spinster and very strict. In the course of time I moved to higher classes and, eventually, was transferred to the boys' section.

The headmaster at the time was Mr Webby and the headmistress was Miss Agget, who was assisted by Miss Pengelly who, after her retirement, married Mr J.J. Shepperd the jeweller. Other teachers I remember were Miss Ada Deane and her married sister Mrs Huntley. On Mr Webby's retirement the new headmaster was Mr Barnes. He had two sons at the school, Norman and Jack, who later went to Allhallows. Mr Barnes was called up during the First World War and was replaced by a Mr Luxton from Ottery St Mary, although Mr Barnes resumed as headmaster when he came back after hostilities had ceased. Another master was Mr Harold Campbell, who to me was one of the finest men I have ever met. He was the organist and choirmaster at St Paul's Church for a great number of years and, naturally he had the pick of the school for his choir, in which I sang for many years.

Some of the classrooms were very dark because the only daylight came from small windows situated near the roof. The only other lighting was from gaslights hanging from the roof. The heating was very poor. This was because it came from heated water pipes on the back wall that were screened off by matchboard screen and the only pupils that were warm were those at the back of the class. I was lucky enough to be one of those.

Some of the boys I remember from my class were Bill Goddard (Honiton Bottom), Bill Lock (Copper Castle), Victor Greenslade, Ernest Rattenbury, Jim Ayres, Johnny Cox, Norman Thomas, Fred Gale, Eddie Riggs, Frank Major, Cyril Evans, Walter Strawbridge, Harry Webber, Tom and Walter Stamp, Harry Dunsford, Peter Dart, Charlie 'Dapper' Moore, Ping Sparks, Bernard Cowling, Maurice Trace, Victor and Percy White (their father was the manager of the old gasworks), and finally Ron and Fred Furzey. Some of the boys and girls came from the workhouse (mostly orphans).

There were no organised sports of any kind and our playground was covered with gravel – this caused many cut hands and knees. The toilets were situated at the far end of the playground and in inclement weather this was not too pleasant. Our pastimes were marbles and hoops and tops.

Empire Day was celebrated every year and the whole school was assembled in the playground where we all sang songs connected with the Empire. Sometimes this took part in the old Fair Field.

These were the days of real poverty and some children came to school very badly dressed and with clothes and footwear many sizes too large.

I left the old school in 1919 and spent four years at the King's School at Ottery St Mary before finishing my schooling at Allhallows.

One person I must mention is the school cleaner, a widow called Mrs Gollop who lived with her son, Harry, a local postman. She came to the school every night and always wore a man's cap, her hair was always in a bun and she also wore an apron made from sacking. She was a real worker and her job was to brush the classrooms each night. Where would you find such a person today?

Families were much larger in my younger days. The Hellier family consisted of eight children – Len, John, Margery, Dorothy, Ruth, Linda, Muriel and Joan. Their father was a saddler and in later years started the Honiton Garage. The Pavey family consisted of nine children, some of who are still living [1988].

One girl that I particularly remember was Jean Soper. Her father was a postman and lived in one of the cottages opposite the National School at the end of Lamb Yard. She later went to King's School at Ottery St Mary and, after leaving school worked for some years at Brockway's, the newsagents in High Street. Another girl I remember was Margery Hales whose father was the manager of the Pearl Assurance Company for many years. Margery married Charlie Selway who later ran a plumbing business in King Street.

When I was about ten years old I was operated on together with two others, George Hartnell and Vera Sparks, for the removal of my tonsils. Two local doctors – Dr Ash and Dr Hedden – did it in the old Black Lion Hotel on the dining-room table. Several hours later I was driven home in the Dolphin Hotel Horse Bus by Mr Norman (senr), the father of Bill Norman. Vera Sparks married Tommy Isaacs and kept the Volunteer and Railway inns. The Black Lion is now demolished together with some adjoining properties.

When the new schools were built the National School was closed in 1940 and it became the workshop and builders' yard of H.E. Hansford & Son.

Margaret Robson remembers her early years in Honiton:

I left my home, the Kennels, Monkton, one January morning to start school with my brother, Clifford, probably in 1931. I remember my mother coming into the lane to wave me off and I walked the two miles, grumbling all the time. I think I must have been a late starter as the dentist was there that day – I cannot imagine that the powers that be would be so cruel as to have him on the first day of term.

I cannot remember Miss Crispin greeting me but I can remember that dentist pushing a box-shaped thing into my mouth and I was furious. I was to hate his visits ever after and always screamed and shouted each time I had to queue with the other children outside the rear cloakroom... [I could] hear the other children screaming inside. He once did get as far as drilling a hole in my tooth before throwing me out of his horrendous-looking chair. Our mum, after a lot of begging and pleading, wrote a note saying that she would take me to a local dentist when necessary. I had the awful humiliation of the teacher reading that letter out to the class pointing that mum had spelt necessary wrongly. I never told her though; she would have been very upset. Anyway, after a lot of abscesses and pain I did have all my teeth out when I was 29 years old. It goes to show what a dreadful experience the visit of the school dentist was in those days; I was and still am terrified of all dentists.

I sat beside Mary Waterhouse on my first day at school and we have remained firm friends for the rest of our lives.

Miss Crispin taught me nursery rhymes and how to count. She had taught my brother and sisters, Clifford, Edna, Dolly, and Joyce, and later was to teach Leslie and also my children, Janet and Carol, and, for a short time, Clifford's boys for the short time they went to school in Honiton.

The classrooms had pot-bellied stoves which belched out great clouds of smoke but, unless they were red hot (and therefore dangerous) not a bit of heat came out. Miss Crispin used to put water in a saucepan on the stove at about eleven o'clock and by about noon it was hot enough to make us country children a cup of cocoa.

The lighting in the middle of the classroom was on both ends of a gas jet – it fascinated me. It was not put on until the last minutes of the day unless absolutely necessary, when prayers were said and an evening hymn sung and I was always keen to go home, yet it always seemed to be dark walking the two miles home, a daunting thing when you think of it. A bus left Honiton at five o'clock but I could be home by then if I walked. The traffic was not as bad as it is today but there were still quite a few large lorries and I had to jump in the hedge to get out of their way.

Miss Lee, the headmistress, was always popping in and out of the classrooms and took a real interest in all her charges. She said, 'These children should not have to come to school so cold and tired, we cannot expect them to learn.' Many children came hungry too; I took bread and butter and banana sandwiches for years. I suppose bananas were cheap and in any case very nourishing. I thought I was a cut above the children who brought bread with no butter and an apple, but below those who brought chicken sandwiches wrapped in greaseproof paper.

Miss Holloway was the first-aid teacher and was called upon to dress any wounds after anyone fell in the playground, which was very often. It was a dreadful place, with potholes all over – how the children were able to play sport there no one will ever know.

One room was divided between two classes, one of them run by Miss Salter. She would come in and put her coat, hat and gloves on her desk and woe betide if it was not put on hangers by the time assembly was called. And we were not allowed into the classroom unless it was absolutely bucketing down with rain, which meant it was a great rush for all of us to get this task done. She rapped my knuckles with a pencil and to this day I can still feel it.

Miss Reader had the other half of the classroom and dividing the school were some steps that led to Miss Ebdon's class and on to Miss Lee's, who was the head teacher. Each child on its birthday was asked to stand on the top of these steps and the following song was sung to them:

> Comes a happy birthday once a year,
> Happy day, one happy day,
> Through the sunshine, through the rain,
> Comes a birthday once again.

During one poetry lesson, when each child had to say a verse from a poem in turn, Bill Salter was sucking the top of his torch, the type with a large magnified top, when his turn came and he swallowed the top. What a panic; someone was sent to Holmes Bakery to get a stale bun, which he was made to swallow in large lumps, and all the class sat in wonder trying to see if the top was going into his stomach. All was well a few days later.

When the girls entered the senior school the sewing lessons became a bit more interesting. We all had to make our own sewing bags to hold our sewing. We decorated them and also put our initial on them, thus revealing our first names because the teachers sometimes used our second or even third names. My initials were M.A.P. so I came in for a lot of teasing. That took about a year and then I had to make a duster; doll's teeth was the size of the stitch I needed I was told, not the massive dog's tooth size I was using. That also took nearly a year then one day I became an auntie to a little boy and I asked if I could make a romper suit for him. 'How old is he?' said Miss Ninnis. 'Three days' I proudly replied. Miss Ninnis took one look at me, cut out an enormous shape twice, made a slit for the neck, and I was away.

The King Street Primary School's infant class in 1907. Left to right, back row: *Charlie Manley, ? Cowling, Leslie Pidgeon, ?, R. Lock, Minnie Sluggett, Austin Dean, ?;* third row: *Ralph Connett, ? Dunn, ?, Fred Lemon, ?, Dick Harris, ? Cowling, Tom Isaacs;* second row: *Bert Evans, ?, Bill Chown, Eileen Thomas, Jack Prewer, Gladys Harris, D. Clapp, May Hartnell;* front row: *George Sparkes, ?, ?, F. Hoyle, ?, ?, Syd Connett, Olive Howard.*

Left: *King Street Primary School, Honiton, c.1930.*

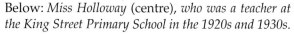

Below: *Miss Holloway* (centre), *who was a teacher at the King Street Primary School in the 1920s and 1930s.*

The former King Street Primary School that was closed in 1940. At the time of this 1960s picture H.E. Hansford & Co., a local builder, occupied it. It was later developed as sheltered housing.

A King Street Primary School sewing class in 1920. The teacher at the back is Miss Salter; among the pupils are Jessie Bambury, Kit Spurway, Kathleen Lewis and Edna Phelps. Of interest, and unusually so for that time, the little girl second from the left in the front is wearing a wristwatch.

Left: *Not a chip in sight, c.1995, when Shirley Stamp served up her last Christmas lunches at Honiton Community College where she had been on the kitchen staff for 26 years. Also pictured is head teacher Norman Tyson.*

Below: *Two 17-year-old Young Enterprise Award students at Honiton Community College, c.1996. Left to right: Sarah Elliman, Miles Rogers (co-ordinator), Alison Edwards.*

Left: *Some of the students at Honiton Community College in 1991 who held a sponsored cycle ride to raise money to build an adventure playground for the disabled.*

No sewing machine, it was all done by hand and after several weeks of doing a run and fall seam across the shoulders, I had to put binding around the neck, including the slit. That binding was put on and taken off so many times that the neck had to be cut bigger and bigger and frayed so that it looked crumpled. To cut a long story short I think that by the time he was three he put it on to have his photo taken.

I also remember that the outbreak of the Second World War meant school started late that term because the evacuees had arrived and were distributed before I was called back, and then it was only mornings so we had to cram a lot of work in. The evacuees had the school in the afternoon. I believe there was some animosity between the town children and the evacuees but I was at home by then.

Mr Griffiths was a member of the British Legion and came one day with labels and lots of names and asked us to write the names of Honiton men in uniform as they were sent cigarettes. He called out the names and asked if anyone knew them, one girl had three brothers on the list.

There follow Keith Eddey's memories of the King Street Primary School:

I lived in the Honiton Police Station where my father was the Police Sergeant from 1935 to 1941. As a result I attended the school from 1935 until I was transferred to Ottery King's School on a scholarship.

I kept in correspondence with Miss Lee until her death. She lived at Awliscombe in the School House there. There was no nonsense with her; a child who was heard swearing was threatened with a soapy mouthwash. Miss Ebdon and Miss Crispin I met in later years in Sidmouth whence they retired. I believe Miss Ebdon was killed tragically in a car crash there. Another teacher I remember was Miss Holloway; a very substantial lady who inspired much affection – she came to see me at home when I had measles.

My special friend was Eric White from Combe Raleigh who was a day older than me. After this lapse of time I am a bit thin on names but I do recall a Bruce Bright, Peter and Gordon Gosling, Eddie Marks, Lawrence Gillard, Dulcie Hawkins, Irene Lake, Doreen Dare, Douglas Pulman, Gordon (?) Manley, Gerald Wilson, Dennis Hill and Leslie and George Pritchard. I remember that Doreen and Irene came to a birthday party at the police station and my mother always remembered the boys having a contest to see who could eat the most sandwiches.

The old police station was a strange building. I read somewhere that it had been a coaching inn; the house at the back where we lived was peculiar in that it was one large room on the ground floor with three doors at the far end – to the larder, upstairs and the scullery. Next door were the cells. A few years ago I bought a postcard of the lower end of High Street showing the police station with sandbags blocking the windows during the war. I sat on the railings outside on 3 September 1939 and went in to hear Neville Chamberlain's speech to the nation saying that war had been declared on Germany. I also sat there and watched the fire-engines go through to Plymouth. The war brought the Durham Light Infantry to Heathfield – what a football team! Later the Royal Ulster Rifles were there, and turning out the pubs was no joke.

I can just remember the Horse Fair across the road and Wyatt's halfpenny tray of sweets; I had a terrible time choosing. I remember the single policemen lodging at the guest-house, the pannier and cattle markets, Hooks the butchers, the dairy near the Devonia cinema – what excitement, 3d. (just over 2½p) on a Saturday morning and with wonderful films.

In 1820 Charles Tucker offered the church (St Michael's) the plot of land in Hind Street (now King Street) on which in later years King Street Primary School would stand before it was replaced by Homelace House, a block of flats whose foundation–stone was laid by the mayor, Walt Summers, a former pupil, on 17 March 1987.

A National School was marked on a map of 1843 as being in Dowell Street where the Boy Scout headquarters are in 2005. But but it was certainly not a National School in the later sense of the word. That term came into existence after the Forster Education Act of 1870, in which William Forster, born at Bradpole near Bridport in 1819, created the national system of compulsory elementary education in England. Such schools were Church of England orientated with much emphasis on the scriptures and regular visits from the local rector or vicar, and Honiton was no exception. There exists a list of the 69 pupils at King Street Primary School who took the scripture exam on 4 March 1874.

The *Honiton Deanery Magazine* of 1891 records that Mr Webby, the headmaster of the boy's school, received an inkstand on his birthday. That year parents were reminded that the summer holidays started on 17 July and that school would reopen on 10 August. The new term saw 127 boys at the school, 114 girls and 128 infants.

Most pupils would make sure they were back for the new term – the annual treat of the Sunday and day-schools took place on the following Wednesday. As many as 480 children (around 100 more than were on the register – perhaps some of last year's pupils had 'rejoined' for the day!) assembled with their banners and marched to St Paul's Church for a short service by the rector, Revd Michael Ferrebee Sadler. After the service the children marched through the town behind the Volunteer Band to a field lent by Mr Pyle. Tea was enjoyed at four o'clock (it must have been a mammoth task preparing the food) and cricket, football, rounders and racing followed. The

Honiton Primary School leavers pose before moving to the senior school in 1994.

Above: *The new extension to Honiton Primary School that was opened in September 1994.*

Left: *Derek Yates, seen on the right, who was headmaster at Honiton Community College for 21 years, is pictured with his successor, Norman Tyson, who took over after Easter 1993.*

The Manor House School orchestra rehearsing for the school Christmas carol service in 1994.

day ended with three cheers for the rector and the teachers, the latter having tea provided for them at the Rectory by Miss Sadler.

Manor House School, standing just below the brow of the hills to the east of Honiton off the A35, began life in Seaton at the Manor House to where Malvern House School for Girls was evacuated from Lewisham during the Second World War. In 1956 the headmistress, Mrs Feare, decided to split the school, keeping approximately 25 boys at Manor House and the girls and small boys were taken to Lynwood, a house on the Beer Road overlooking the Chine. Eventually both schools were closed, but they were reopened on 18 September 1958 at Manor House by Francis Eyles, formerly headmaster at Beer Primary School, and his wife Mary. There were 55 pupils there. At the time the school fees were:

Kindergarten	*£12.12.0d. a term (£12.60)*
Seven and over	*£15.15.0d. a term (£15.75)*
Ten and over	*£20.18.0d. a term (£20.90)*
13 and over	*£25.2.0d. a term (£20.20)*

As some of the pupils were approaching 15 years of age, O-level courses had to be taught. Two years later Mr Eyles decided to operate Manor House as a preparatory school with four full-time teachers: Francis and Mary Isles, Miss V. Mellor and Mrs A. Andrews, along with one or two part-time teachers.

So successful was the school that it was unable to cope with the number of pupils seeking admission and Mr Eyles bought Springfield House, Honiton, a property built by Mr A.J. Luxton, whose granddaughters, Rebecca and Beth, would one day become pupils.

Before being opened as a school the house, divided into flats, had to be adapted into classrooms. Fire safety equipment was installed, a 750-feet main sewer was dug and a fleet of minibuses purchased. The dining-hall at Seaton, still in use today as the Folly Nursery, was dismantled and re-erected at Springfield and the school moved in September using horseboxes, tractors and trailers, cars and trailers, lorries and even some parents' cars. The first term in the school's new home began on 1 October 1969 with 99 children on the roll.

Since then the school has grown considerably. A new laboratory has been built, and sports are held on Midsummer Meadow, the triangular field opposite the Bishop's Tower. A music room, sports hall and brick sports pavilion have also been built.

Other recent changes include the creation of an ICT/library suite in one of the former residential flats, new kitchens and dining facilities. In the grounds the new features include a millennium mosaic, a willow sculpture and a nursery playground. Another change saw a new uniform make its appearance.

Peter Eyles took over as headmaster in around 1986 until the Eyles family sold the school to Geoffrey and Mary Ann Wilmot in 1998 when Simon Bage, Peter Eyles's deputy, was appointed headmaster.

Above: *Junior pupils at Manor House School in 2004.*

Above right: *Pupils of Honiton Primary School singing carols at Honiton Library on 20 December 1993, as part of a Christmas programme by schoolchildren throughout East Devon.*

Right: *The Devon Air Ambulance pays a 'Thank You' visit to Manor House School in 2000 after receiving a donation. Standing with his back to the camera, in a change from being behind one, is Colin Bowerman, cameraman for* Pulman's Weekly News *and* The Honiton Advertiser.

Alderman A.F. Studley presenting the Freeman of the Borough board to the mayor in the Council Chambers in 1960. The picture includes: John Halse, Reg Thomas (behind), Walt Summers, Arthur Real, Alderman Tucker (mayor), Joe Lake (town crier), Mr A.F. Studley.

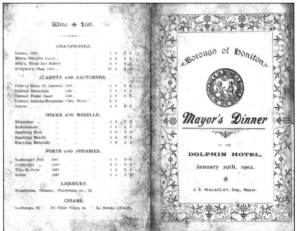

Right: *The outside covers on the Mayor's Dinner programme. The event was held by the mayor, Mr J.C. McCaulay, on 19 January 1902. The wine list will cause a few nostalgic, even sad, sighs with good some wines going at four shillings (25p).*

Honiton Town Council in 2002. Left to right, back row: Michael Teare, Ken Joy, Ron Webb, Roger Sleeman, Ken Hopkins, Richard Howe, Revd Peter Robinson; middle row: Marcella Boot, Vera Howard, Marion Olive, Sally Casson, Dave Retter (town crier); seated: Mike Smith, George Robson, Ruth Robson (mayor), Helen Curtis.

Chapter 7

Honiton's Mayors

The port reeve, appointed by the lord of the manor, was both the magistrate of the court and the returning officer for the borough and, because of his debt to the lord of the manor, he was usually able to secure a seat for his protégé in a two-seat borough such as Honiton. This was the prime cause for the development of the rotten boroughs that existed until the Municipal Corporation Act of 1832, which established a uniform system of government in boroughs.

Honiton became a municipal borough on 17 November 1846 with a council consisting of a mayor, six aldermen and 18 councillors. It was to remain a borough until 1972 when the Local Government Act abolished boroughs and a town council served Honiton. The last borough mayor was Mr H.H. Black in 1973, the first town mayor, the following year, was Mr T.H. Hitchcock. Honiton's first mayor was Christopher Flood, who was elected in 1847 following the first council election on 1 February that year.

HONORARY FREEMEN OF THE BOROUGH OF HONITON

Cyril Neville Tweed	20 Feb 1936
Mrs Juanita Maxwell Tweed	10 Feb 1938
Air Chief Marshall Sir Arthur Harris	23 July 1945
Harold Ernest Carnell	1 Oct 1945
Albert Frederick Studley	23 Oct 1953
F.W.C. Tucker	4 April 1972

HONOURED CITIZENS

William Cogger	13 Jan 2002
Walter Summers	13 Jan 2002

FOR THE
INFORMATION OF THE RATE-PAYERS
OF THE BOROUGH OF HONITON.

VOTING FOR THE TOWN CLERK'S SALARY.—

Moved by CAPT. BASLEIGH, and seconded by MR. WOODWARD, that the Town Clerk's Salary be Fifty Pounds a Year.

Moved by MR. COX, and seconded by MR. TOWNSEND, that the Salary be Thirty Pounds a Year.

FOR FIFTY POUNDS A YEAR.	FOR THIRTY POUNDS A YEAR.
THE MAYOR	MR. JERRARD
CAPT. BASLEIGH	MR. COX
MR. WOODWARD	CAPT. GROUBE
MR. PLAYER	MR. STAMP
MR. DAVEY	MR. REED
MR. AVERY	MR. Mc. KNO
MR. LEE	MR. BAKER
MR. MURCH	MR. WHEATON
	MR. DENNER
	MR. MELHUISH
	MR. TOWNSEND.

MR. WOODGATES, MR. HOLLAND and MR. PEAKE were present and did not Vote.

Moved by CAPT. BASLEIGH, and seconded by MR. WOODWARD, that the Town Clerk's Salary be Forty Pounds a Year.

FOR FORTY POUNDS A YEAR.	FOR THIRTY POUNDS A YEAR.
THE MAYOR	MR. JERRARD
CAPT. BASLEIGH	MR. COX
MR. WOODWARD	CAPT. GROUBE
MR. REED	MR. STAMP
MR. WOODGATES	MR. Mc. KNO
MR. PLAYER	MR. BAKER
MR. DAVEY	MR. WHEATON
MR. AVERY	MR. DENNER
MR. LEE	MR MELHUISH
MR. PEAKE	MR. TOWNSEND
MR. MURCH	

MR. HOLLAND was present and did not Vote.   MR. BISHOP was absent from the Council.

I publish the above in order that the Rate-payers may see who Vote away the Public money in large Salaries which they will have to pay by another Rate.

A COUNCILLOR.

KNIGHT, PRINTER, HONITON.

The mayor, Walt Summers, unveils the foundation-stone at the new Homelace House apartments for the retired, prior to 1978–79. With him are Peter Wilson, contracts manager for the developers, McCarthy & Son, and Joe Lake, the town crier.

Borough Mayors

C. Flood/J.H. Townsend	1847	J.C. McCaulay	1901
J. Basleigh	1848	J.C. McCaulay	1902
R.H. Aberdein	1849	J.C. McCaulay	1903
W. Woodward	1850	J. Knowles	1904
E. Stamp	1851	J. Knowles	1905
J.C. Jerrard	1852	H. Banfield	1906
J. Basleigh	1853	H. Banfield	1907
R.H. Aberdein	1854	C.N. Tweed	1908
S. Devenish	1855	C.N. Tweed	1909
E. Stamp	1856	S.W. Hook	1910
S.M. Cox	1857	S. Cox	1911
R.H. Aberdein	1858	R.H. Matthews	1912
J.C. Jerrard	1859	R.H. Matthews	1913
E.Stamp	1860	R.H. Matthews	1914
J.C. Jerrard	1861	R.H. Matthews	1915
J. Ashley	1862	C.N. Tweed	1916
J.C. Jerrard	1863	C.N. Tweed	1917
M. Murch	1864	S.W. Hook	1918
J. Ashley/M. Murch	1865	S.W. Hook	1919
J. Knight	1866	Mrs J.M. Phillips	1920
D. Gould	1867	Mrs J.M. Phillips	1921
G.T. Tweed	1868	Mrs J.M. Phillips	1922
E. Stamp	1869	Mrs J.M. Phillips	1923
R.P. Harrison	1870	H.R. Matthews	1924
G. White	1871	Mrs J.M. Phillips	1925
J. Read	1872	E.W. Matthews	1926
J. Ashley	1873	E.W. Matthews	1927
H. Fowler	1874	E.W. Matthews	1928
J.S. Swann	1875	F.L. Courtenay	1929
H. Lee	1876	F.L. Courtenay	1930
J. Knight	1877	F.L. Courtenay	1931
F.C. Glanville	1878	F.L. Courtenay	1932
H. Fowler	1879	W.A.E. Stamp	1933
H. Hook	1880	C.N. Tweed	1934
H. Hook	1881	E.H. Brock	1935
M. Murch	1882	Mrs J.M. Phillips	1936
H. Fowler	1883	Mrs J.M. Phillips	1937
J.C. McCaulay	1884	Mrs J.M. Phillips	1938
C. Read	1885	Mrs J.M. Phillips	1939
D.W.R. Buchanan	1886	Mrs J.M. Phillips	1940
J.C. McCaulay	1887	A.F. Studley	1941
C. Read	1888	A.F. Studley	1942
H. Hook	1889	C.N. Hatcher	1943
C. Harding	1890	C.N. Hatcher	1944
C. Read	1891	Mrs J.M. Phillips	1945
T.B. Avery	1892	R.R.K. Marker	1946
D.W.R. Buchanan	1893	H.R. Real	1947
J.C. McCaulay	1894	H.R. Real	1948
D.W.R. Buchanan	1895	H.R. Real	1949
H. Banfield	1896	W.J. Durbin	1950
D.W.R. Buchanan	1897	W.J. Durbin	1951
R.H. Matthews	1898	R.R.K. Marker	1952
R.H. Matthews	1899	R.J. Cann	1953
R.H. Matthews	1900	R.J. Cann	1954

R.J. Cann	1955	T.H. Steel	1965
W.J.R. Board	1956	A.G. Real	1966
W.J.R. Board	1957	A.G. Real	1967
W.J.R. Board	1958	R.B. Thorne	1968
F.W.C. Tucker	1959	R.B. Thorne	1969
F.W.C. Tucker	1960	S.J. Stone	1970
F.W.C. Tucker	1961	S.J. Stone	1971
Dr A.T.H. Glanvill	1962	H.H. Black	1972
H.E.Hansford	1963	H.H. Black	1973
H.E. Hansford	1964		

TOWN MAYORS

T.H. Hitchcock	1974	P.G. Blake	1990
R.L. Gigg	1975	P.G. Blake	1991
R.L. Gigg	1976	Dr A.T.H. Glanvill	1992
Dr A.T.H. Glanvill	1977	R.J. Shepherd	1993
Dr A.T.H. Glanvill	1978	R.J. Shepherd	1994
M.L. Stone	1979	Mrs J. Bull	1995
M.L. Stone	1980	Mrs J. Bull	1996
M.L. Stone	1981	Mrs J. Bull	1997
A.J. Dimond	1982	R.M.P. Howe	1998
P.A. Allen	1983	R.M.P. Howe	1999
P.A. Allen	1984	R.A. Sharpe	2000
W.E. Cogger	1985	Mrs R. Robson	2001
A.W. Summers	1986	Mrs R. Robson	2002
A.W. Summers	1987	Mrs H. Curtiss	2003
R. Walker	1988	Mrs S. Casson	2004
A. Walker	1989		

For many years the position of macebearer and town crier was virtually a fiefdom of the Lake family being held in turn by Joseph Lake senr, his son Joseph John, and his grandsons Tom and Joe.

In May 1997 the local press reported that Mrs J. Bull had voted herself into an unprecedented third term of office as mayor. But they were overlooking that fact that Mrs Juanita Maxwell Phillips had served as mayor for as many as 11 terms, five terms in a row between 1936–40 and four in a row between 1920–23. Mr Frederick Leslie Courtenay served for four successive years (1929–32); Mr R.H. Matthews served for four terms (1912–15) after having served earlier for three in a row (1898–1900). Also Mr J.C. McCaulay (1901–03), Mr R.J. Cann (1953–55) and Mr W.J.R. Board (1956–58) served three successive terms. The press did, however, correctly say that the mayor choosing ceremony 'went anything but smoothly'. A first ballot saw Mrs Bull get six votes and Mr Sharpe and Mrs Olive four each. Mrs Olive lost the fight for second place on the toss of a coin. In the second ballot Mr Sharpe won 7–6 until someone pointed out that there was a missing ballot paper. It turned out to be Mrs Bull's who, naturally, had voted for herself, and the ballot was now a 7–7 tie and Mrs Bull used her casting vote to return herself as mayor for the third term. She also won a vote of confidence 7–0 with seven abstentions, which surely means that she must have voted for herself again.

Sally Casson, mayor of Honiton in 2004.

The Honiton Royal Mail Post Bus outside Dunkeswell Post Office in the 1970s. The first of its kind to be operated in England, the service started on 23 October 1967. As well as carrying passengers to Luppitt and other villages in the Luppitt area, it delivered to and collected mail from Post Offices in those villages.

Linda Pridmore and Paul Cann, the two drivers, pictured on a card produced to mark the 25th anniversary of the Honiton Royal Mail Post Bus service on 23 October 1992 at Honiton Bottom.

The Post Office

Since the eighteenth century, there had been a charge of one penny to cover the cost of the journey from the receiving house to the Post Office and the letter was usually, but not always, hand-stamped to show that the penny had been paid. Naturally, the local system, by which the outlying villages of Luppitt, Dunkeswell, Gittisham, Awliscombe and so on, sent their mail to the Post Office at Honiton was known as the Honiton Penny Post. It was not unique to Honiton; almost every small town that had a Post Office and served its smaller neighbours operated a penny post. It follows therefore that there was an Axminster Penny Post, a Sidmouth Penny Post and so on.

Many people confuse the Penny Post with the universal postal system introduced by Sir Rowland Hill in May 1840 because of the Penny Black stamp that was introduced at the same time – certainly until at least 1998 *The New Oxford English Dictionary* did so. Sir Rowland Hill's new postal arrangement did not herald in a universal penny charge on letters, only on the first weight step; heavy letters cost more.

A foot postman delivered the mail for the villages on their outward journeys and, in the case of the Luppitt area, he spent the rest of the day in a small hut on Luppitt Common before collecting the mail at Luppitt Post Office and walking back to Honiton.

Honiton's mail either reached or left the town by four different types of posts – London letters, country letters, cross-post letters and bye-letters. The first group is self explanatory – letters that travelled direct to or from the capital. 'Country' letters passed through London on their way to their final destination – say Honiton to Norwich. As the name suggests, a cross post was one that went 'across country' and did not touch London on its way from one provincial town to another – for example Honiton–Taunton–Bristol, Dorchester–Bristol, Exeter–Cardiff and many others. Bye-letters travelled along the main coach runs without getting as far as London – from Honiton again to, say, Salisbury or Andover.

The number of miles a letter had to travel from Honiton determined the charge for conveying and delivering both the letters from the outlying villages and those posted directly into the system at Honiton. Before the introduction of the Universal Post and the postage stamp the charges were considerable, although the rate tended to be lowered for longer distances. Thus, although a letter from Honiton to Dorchester cost about six pence, one to London cost around a shilling.

In 1850 the Post Office was in High Street with Richard Taylor as postmaster. Letters were despatched to London and all other parts at 7.15p.m., to Dorchester and Bridport at 5.20p.m. and to Sidmouth at 6a.m. and a 6.50p.m.

Wall boxes began to arrive in Honiton in around the 1880s and by 1900 John Soper was one of the first postmen in the town to deliver the mail by bicycle, operating one with solid tyres at first. It was around that time that a Mr Doble drove by horse and cart to meet the mail train at Cullompton and returned to Honiton at 4a.m. Honiton's first two motor delivery vans arrived in 1926.

A record that would be hard to beat came when two Honiton postmen brothers retired in 1959 after a combined service of 95 years. Ernest Connett started work with the Post Office in 1910 when he was paid five shillings as a messenger boy, plus two pence a day for cleaning the cycle that he used. He went on to drive one of the last horse-drawn mail coaches that took the mail to Stockland, where he had a reputation for being so punctual that when he was making a collection people set their watches by him. During the First World War he served with the 2/4th Devons in India and Turkey. He retired a few days before his brother as a higher-grade postman. His brother Donald followed him into the Post Office in 1913 and after the First World War was a postman at Axminster for a spell. He became a higher-grade postman and was made assistant inspector in Honiton in 1957. He also played football and rugby for Honiton.

This postcard is marked 'High Street 1920' on the reverse and it is possible that this is a parade of the Honiton Comrades of the Great War. The men certainly have a military bearing.

The Exe Group of Devon branches of the British Legion pass the saluting dias as they march to St Paul's Church for a combined service in the 1950s.

The British Legion Band heads the 1958 Remembrance Day Parade as it marches up High Street towards St Paul's Church. The former Read's garage is on the left.

HONITON BRANCH

Annual Dinner

Turk's Head Cafe

Saturday, March 5th, 1949

GRACE

REV. H. T. HILLIER (Branch Chaplain)

DINNER

Toast List

"H.M. THE KING"

Proposed by THE PRESIDENT

"THE BRITISH LEGION"

Proposed by HIS WORSHIP THE MAYOR
(Councillor H. R. READ, J.P.)

Responded to by T. B. REVILL, ESQ.
(County Chairman)

"HONITON BRANCH BRITISH LEGION"

Proposed by BRIG. GUY BARRINGTON
(Chairman, Axminster Branch)

Responded to by CAPT. B. R. DUNNING
(Branch President)

"THE VISITORS"

Proposed by LT.-GEN. E. A. OSBORNE
(Vice-President)

Responded to by C.O. HEATHFIELD CAMP
(COL. J. A. SAMUEL, R.E.M.E.)

"ACT OF REMEMBRANCE"

LAST POST

INVOCATION

MR. L. A. PAVEY (Branch Chairman)

REVEILLE

CHEQUERS CONCERT PARTY

Chapter Nine
The Royal British Legion

In Flanders Fields

In Flanders fields the poppies blow
Between the crosses row on row,
That mark our place: and in the sky
The larks, still bravely singing, fly
Scarce heard amid the guns below

We are the dead. Short days ago
We lived, felt dawn, saw sunset glow,
Loved and were loved, and now we lie
In Flanders Fields

Take up our quarrel with the foe;
To you from failing hands we throw
The torch: be yours to hold it high
If ye break faith with us who die
We shall not sleep, though Poppies grow
In Flanders fields.

Written in May 1915 at the second battle of Ypres by
Lt Col John McCrae – he died in January 1918.

Honiton, like many other towns in Devon, was offered a German field gun to be placed in a central position in the town after the end of the First World War. At the same time (January 1920) the question of a suitable memorial to the men of the town who had been killed in action was causing lively debate. Some wanted a memorial hall or playing-field, others a granite obelisk or cross which would have the names of the fallen and, strangely and not done, those who had served overseas. This might have added quite a lot to the cost, as many Honiton men served with the Devonshire Regiment in Mesopotamia as well as with the BEF in France. Although the men of the town who had served in the Forces were generally in favour of something other than a memorial obelisk or cross, that was the course that was adopted and, in due time, the memorial was placed in front of the parish church.

Mrs Phillips was the mayor in 1921 when she officially unveiled the war memorial on 14 July in the presence of:

... a large and representative gathering that included the members of the Corporation, the Territorials, in charge of Lieutenant Batten, the Comrades of the Great War, under Major-General Cookson, special constables,

Girl Guides, the staff and members of Honiton VAD Hospital, the Honiton War Hospital, moss pickers for the Hospital, sandbag makers and the comforts committee.

On the side facing the street is the inscription:

To the men of Honiton whose names are inscribed and to their comrades who gave their lives in the war 1914–19. Remember them with honour and thanksgiving.

On the side facing the church are the words: 'Christ also suffered for us, leaving us an example that we should follow in his steps.'

The names on the war memorial are:

1914–19

W. Ackland	P.C. Bowden
R.R. Bromfield	R.J. Broom
H. Brown	F. Buckingham
E. Burrough	F. Channon
W. Channon	W.J. Clarke
C. Dean	W.C. Densham
E.R. Dimond	A.J. Dunn
P. Durbin	S.C. Durbin
W. Edwards	J. Evans
F.C. Gigg	F.W. Gill
W.C. Gollop	W. Gould
R.M. Harenburg	R.F. Harris
E.C. Hawkins	W.J. Hooper
H.C. Kallaway	E. Knight
R.P. Knowles	G. Lake
H.T. Langelan	W. Larcombe
A.E. Lawrence	S.E.C. Lock
J.B. Lucas	T. Marshall
C.A.G. Perryman	F. Pope
A.G. Power	A.W. Power
W.J. Prewer	E.E. Proll
A.E. Rabjohns	E.L. Radford
G.B. Ramsbotham	W.J. Riggs
H. White	S.P.W. Rowland
A.C. Sansom	W.E. Snow
W.S. Stone	F.G. Strawbridge
G. Summers	B.J. Tucker
R.G. Tucker	J.G.W. Tweed
F. Vosper	G.H. Ward
W.H. Warr	W.B. Webb
F. Weed	H. White
W.J. Wills	F.J. Wood
W.J. Wood	E. Wyatt

Dr Terry Glanvill, Honiton Royal British Legion Club president laying a wreath at the war memorial on Remembrance Sunday in the 1960s.

1939–45

C.H. Baulch	L. Boyland
E.C. Cursons	R.W. Densham
E.R. Dimond	P.R. Dobbin
D. Edgvean	H. Ford
W.C. Gould	P.C. Greenslade
S.E. Greenslade	J.E.D. Hook
E.C. Marker	A.A. Moon
S.W. Nicholls	W.W. Oliver
E.F. Pope	S.V. Stamp
A. Travers	R.F. Webber

Northern Ireland 1972

G.C. Bristow

Allhallows School has its own altar memorial on which are commemorated the Old Honitonians who gave their lives in the First World War. The altar front was of beaten and golden bronze and was presented to the school by Arthur Chudleigh and members of the Lillies family. Recorded on the memorial are:

The late Dave Lapping, Honiton Royal British Legion Standard Bearer, on parade on Remembrance Day 1988.

A fine body of men. Members of the Honiton branch of the Royal British Legion march to church on an 11 November Armistice Parade in the 1940s/'50s. In those days the church service and wreath-laying ceremony was on 11 November, the anniversary of the day in 1918 when the Armistice was signed. Among members present are: Mr Dunning, Major-General Essame, Mr Hatcher, Arthur Leat, Mr Watson, Major Soanes, Bill Wood, Mr Pavey and Cyril Tucker.

Old Honitonians who died, 1914–18

A.P. Abecasis	D.C.H. Aldsworth
V.J.D. Ascott	H.T. Atay
H.W. Atay DSO	R.F. Barton
J.U. Chisholm-Batten	T.L. Blatchford
G.T. Body	R.M. Brind MC
M.B. Checkland	W.G.E. Clapp
G. Compton	H.W.F. Cooke
J.J. De Gex	M.L. Goldie DSO
A.L. Goldie	E.M. Gould
E.A.N. Hackett	D.W.H. Humphreys DSO
G.G.P. Humphreys	F.C. James
K.L. James	J.D. Key
S.H. Kirby	R.D. Lammert
W.H.F. Landon	F.J. Leach
G. Leather	L.E.T. Lemon
E.G. Lester	C.W. Lydall
J.C. Marson	C.J. McConaghey
G.S. Meddie	R.W. Michell
R.F. Michelmore	A.P. Palmer DSO
E.D. Palmer	A.G. Power
A. Preedy	A.W. Prentice
G.B. Ramsbotham	E.R. Reynolds
T.O. Risdon	J.E. Salter
C.F. Sandoe	M.W.A. Sandoe
C.W. Short MC	R.H. Stranger
F. Street	C.M. Teague
J.C.J. Teague	B.J. Tucker
J.G.W. Tweed	J.M. Tyrell
L.A.H. Tyrell	C.L. Usher
P.W. Ward MC	H.L. Watts
R.K. Watts	W.B. Webb
A.C. Whitaker	H.C.F. White

The names A.B. Power, G.B. Ramsbotham and J.G.W. Tweed appear on both memorials.

It was around this time that the Honiton Comrades of the Great War decided to change their name and status and become members of the newly formed British Legion (later Royal British Legion and, almost invariably, the name used throughout this book).

The field gun arrived in January 1921 and it was the decision of the Town Council to place it at Copper Castle, but it is thought to have been quickly removed because, it is said, 'the people of Honiton did not want to live beneath a German gun.'

The outbreak of the Second World War brought fresh impetus to the sale of poppies on the first wartime Armistice Day in 1939. Almost every village and town in East Devon reported that record amounts had been raised on Poppy Day – Honiton's figure was £120 with some money still to come in, which meant it was well up on the previous record of £95 in 1937.

The Honiton branch of the Royal British Legion had its first HQ in a pub or pubs in the town but it soon acquired the land at the end of Dowell Street, where the present Royal British Legion Club stands, and its own first branch headquarters and club was a wooden building there, constructed largely of light timber and felt. It served the branch faithfully for many years but, in the manner of such things, it had deteriorated to such an extent that the felt roof needed replacing and the walls needed repairing during the 1950s. The club was told that if the building was not renovated immediately it would be closed and the billiards table sold. Cash was short at the time and an appeal was made to members for loans, on which interest of 2.5 per cent would be paid – the amounts advanced to be in multiples of five shillings (25p); £500 was needed. Members were also told that it was intended to repair the hut at the time but plans were afoot to build a permanent HQ on the site if and when the money became available.

Few organisations can match the Royal British Legion in raising money (usually for others), and they put their usual effort into raising cash for a new HQ. It paid off when the new building was opened in 1962. The new bar was in use before the official opening when Dr Terry Glanvill, the club president, pulled the first drink – a pint of beer that was drunk by the mayor, Alderman Tom Steel. Also present were Miss D.S. Dunning, president of the women's section, Mr B.R. Dunning, branch life president, and Mr W. Strawbridge, building committee chairman.

Ten years later, on 31 March 1972, the present larger hall was added and in 2005 the 1,000-member-strong branch continues to flourish both as a social centre for members and as a means of carrying on the work that all Royal British Legion branches exist for – not just 'remembering them' but helping their dependents that are in need of help.

Jim Kendall playing for the Honiton Royal British Legion Band at the Celebration Concert in the Royal British Legion HQ on 4 March 1987.

It was a proud moment for members of the Honiton branch of the Royal British Legion in 1962 when their brand new clubhouse was opened on the site of a previous wooden building at the end of Dowell Street.

Left: *A Christmas concert at the Honiton RBL HQ in 2002. The band members are: (cornets) Lorraine Pavey, Roger Sleaman, Sharon Dibsdale, Kevin Roulson, Rachel Langley; (piano) Kathryn Gibbs, Jack Clarke, Peter Furzey, Richard Brain, Harry Andrews, John Woodland; (flugelhorn) Louise Pavey; (tenor horns) Stephen Childs, Heather Marriner, Ron Marriner; (euphoniums) George Dibsdale, Keith Massam; (baritones) Arthur Dunn, Ian Sleaman; (trombones) N. Conabeare, Jonathan Sleaman, Sam Noad, John Marriot; (bass) Tony Smith, David Lee, Tom Betley, Louise Conabeare; (percussion) Jim Kendall; (bandmaster) Malcolm Avery.*

The Royal British Legion

This Certificate is awarded to Royal British Legion Band, Honiton in grateful recognition of devoted service to the cause of The Royal British Legion in the County of Devon.

President

Chairman

Date 25th November 1989

Hon. Secretary

The official opening of the new Honiton Royal British Legion HQ took place in 1962. Seen here handing over the deeds to the club secretary, Vic Denne, is the branch life president Mr Dunning.

An unknown occasion in the old wooden Honiton Royal British Legion clubhouse in the 1950s. Left to right: Mr Dunning, Mr Watson, and Mr Pavey.

The opening of Royal British Legion Hall on 31 March 1972 by John Stone ARIBA. Left to right: Mr Heapy, Alf Robins, John Stone, the mayor Ron Gigg.

Above: *Honiton Royal British Legion officers and committee members in 1962. Left to right, back row: Bill Elston, ?, ?, Guy Thrupp, ?, Alf Robins, Colin Hunt, ?, ?, Stan Vinnicombe, 'Chillie' Charlton; third row: Len Brooking, Mr Dean, John Stone, Mr James, Reg Gigg, Les Summers, Gordon Lock, Jimmy Robson, Les Moore, ?; second row: ?, John Woodland, Barbara Denne, ?, Margaret Robson, Stella Loveridge, Reg Watts, Bert Channon, Mrs Channon, Bill Strawbridge; front row: ?, Vic Denne, Miss Dunning, Fred Lane, Mr Dunning, Dr Terry Glanvill, Mrs Ridler, Ken Randall, Dudley Todd.*

Left and far left: *Standard Bearers of the Honiton branch of the Royal British Legion in the 1950s were Reg Gigg and Queenie Tozer (women's section).*

Chapter 10
Churches, Chapels and Other Buildings

Rectors of Honiton

Year	Name
1224	Walter
1272	Sir Henry de Montford
1276	Adam Paen
1285	Master Guyde Tillbrok
	Henry de Pykeney
1314	Richard de Wydelsade
1324	Philip de Puntyngtone
1361	Sir John Bysouthdone
1361	Richard Gardiner
1391	Richard Madeford
1399	Edward Ffysche
1408	Robert Fynour
1412	John Sneynton
1433	Thomas Smith
1442	Richard Lawe (or Lowe)
1450	John Rigge (or Rugge)
1459	Thomas Frome
1459	Geoffrey Newchurch
1487	John Melbury
1500	John Yeate
1505	Henry Ferman (or Feyrman)
1527	Richard Denys
1528	Nicholas Courtenay
1540	Philip Bale
1559	Robert Slade
1587	Hugh Dowriche (or Dowrish)
1598	John Robins
1606	Philip Nicholls
1614	John Eedes
1648	Francis Sourton (or Soorten)
1663	Ozias Upcott
1699	Ezra Cleavland
1740	Charles Bertie
1788	Edward Honywood
1813	Henry Allwright Hughes
1827	Villiers Plantaganet Henry Somerset
1855	John Fielder Mackarness
	(later the Bishop of Oxford)
1870	Michael Ferrebee Sadler
1895	Hugh John Fortescue
1908	Frederick Leslie Courtenay
	(later the 16th Earl of Devon)
1935	Andrew Augustine Fane de Salis
1963	Richard Andrew Babington
1972	Robin Mark George Morrell
1978	James William Irvine Trevelyan
2001	Jane Hedges

Revd Jane Hedges, rector of Honiton since 2001.

St Paul's

It is a long walk from High Street up New Street and then Church Hill to St Michael's parish church and as early as 1429 the townspeople of Honiton petitioned the Pope to have mass celebrated in the Chapel of All Saints. They claimed that was because of the 'perils of the roads and on account of the floods of the waters which flow between St Michael's and the town.' However, it was more likely to have been the long, mostly uphill walk that they disliked, something that a chapel of ease would do away with.

The Pope's writ no longer ran in Honiton by the nineteenth century but the walk up to St Michael's was still there and it was just as long and hard, especially for the elderly and infirm. The church was closed in the mid-nineteenth century and the present parish church of St Paul's replaced it.

St Paul's was built in 1835–37 at a cost of £7,600 on the site of the old Allhallows Chapel. Because the size and shape of the land available dictated the orientation of the new church, it unusually if not uniquely, lies north–south and not east–west. The site cost £2,400 and to make room for the church, the chapel was demolished.

What distinguishes it the most is the tall, 104-foot tower, but the church, built of Beer stone with a local chert dressing, is in the Norman style which clashes with the elegant Georgian buildings that grace High Street. The six bells arrived from the Allhallows Chapel in 1836 and the roof of the nave was said to be unsafe, so a new one, 6 feet lower, replaced it in 1965.

In 1936 the Honiton Parochial Church Council accepted an offer of the screen from St Paul's Church,

Honiton Parish Church Choir in 1952. Left to right, back row: Brian Davis, Bill Norman, H. Dean, J. Helliar, Max Pulman, J. Lonsdale, Revd A. Fane de Salis, R. Gillard, L.E. Helliar, E. Sparkes, Don Connett, David Hann; middle row: W.S. Turner, Arthur Real, E. Clapp, Archie Dimond, H.E. Carnell, A. Wyatt, H. Gollop, B. Dyer, W.H. Barnes; front row: Bill Collins, Michael Oliver, Terry Jenkins, B.W. Underwood, D.M. Lane, R.C.S. Matthews, D.C.L. Ely, D.F. Hall, R. Hann, Peter Rattenbury, Barry Pulman.

Left: The view from the tower of St Paul's Church on 19 April 1994. There are plenty of sheep at Honiton Market but, as yet, few buyers. Behind the market is the senior school with the sports hall behind again. Over on the centre background is the swimming-pool with the rugby clubhouse on the left.

Below: Steve Loader watching work on the flagpole of St Paul's Church on 19 April 1994.

Tom Steel, mayor of Honiton, outside St Paul's Church for an occasion in 1955. He had obviously just received something (a cheque?) from Dr Terry Glanvill. Also in the picture are Walt Summers, behind the mayor's right shoulder, Mrs Steel and Joe Lake, the town crier.

Exeter, which was to be demolished under the Union of Benefices Act of 1923. It was transferred and erected in Honiton's St Paul's. It was first seen in its new setting during the evening service on Sunday, 5 April 1936 when the rector, Revd A.A. Fane de Salis, described it as 'a beautiful addition to the church'. Later that year it was announced that parishioners of Honiton were to erect a rood-screen in memory of the late Revd Frederick Leslie Courtenay, who was rector for 27 years before becoming the 16th Earl of Devon.

There are eight bells in the tower – six from the belfry of the Allhallows Chapel that was replaced by St Paul's, and two more were added in 1949. The present organ is the third to have been in the church. The first, of which little is known, was replaced in 1873 by an organ that was erected by Bishop & Son. This in turn was replaced in 1999 by an instrument that has two manuals and pedals with 23 speaking stops, mechanical action to the keyboards and electric stop control.

Considerable restoration work was carried out in 1987, including the rebuilding of the parapet walls on new corbel stones and two new single-sloping lead roofs on the aisles. Inside, the reredos was moved from its position behind the altar to the south aisle. The screen at the west end of the nave was moved to where it is in 2005 and a partition wall was added above, forming a narthex (an antechamber or a distinct area separated off by a railing and used by catechumens, penitents, etc).

An incident among the more amusing trivia in the story of St Paul's occurred in 1937 when the rector, Revd Fane de Salis, was away. His locum, Revd G.L. Dickinson from Heavitree, was accidentally locked in the church on a Saturday morning. He raised the alarm by ringing the bells and Frank Doble, the verger, went to his rescue.

That same year an attempt was launched by the proprietor of the Angel Hotel, Mr R.D. Sprake, to stop

The nave at St Paul's Church in 1910.

the clock chiming at night. His solicitors wrote to the Town Council that 'chiming throughout the night was disturbing his visitors, many of whom refused to come again.' Mr Sprake's solicitors pointed out that the question of the night-time chiming had been raised before and they had been advised then that the chiming did constitute a nuisance. Furthermore, the chiming served no useful purpose. A councillor, Mr Napier, agreed it was a nuisance and that he knew from experience that the parents of pupils at Allhallows School complained regularly, as did many other people who lived in the area.

The Town Council suggested that a referendum be held and that everyone would have a vote, not just those who lived within a quarter-mile of the church, as some councillors thought would be fairer. The suggestion was made that if Mr Sprake paid for the winding of the clock, instead of the council, he could regulate the hours at which it chimed. He paid £20 and the clock did not chime after midnight (Mr Sprake wanted them stopped after 11 o'clock) or until 7.30 in the morning (which Alderman J.R. Bowden thought was too late).

St Michael's

One of the treasures in St Michael's was a beautiful rood-screen that was destroyed by fire in 1911. It was

The exterior of St Paul's Church, c.1990.

Above left: *St Michael's Church from an old print dated around 1800.*

Above: *The lych-gate at St Michael's Church in 1911.*

Left: *The nave, rood-screen and altar at St Michael's Church before the 1911 fire.*

St Michael's Church in 1793.

Looking towards the rood-screen at St Michael's Church in 1880 that, along with most of the other woodwork, was destroyed during the 1911 fire.

The superb rood-screen that was destroyed during the fire at St Michael's Church in 1911.

Above: *The nave at St Michael's Church in 1912, after restoration work following the fire. The seating has been replaced with chairs and there is a single beam in front of the altar instead of the rood-screen.*

Right: *The remains of St Michael's Church after the fire of 26 March 1911.*

Below: *St Michael's Church in the 1950s.*

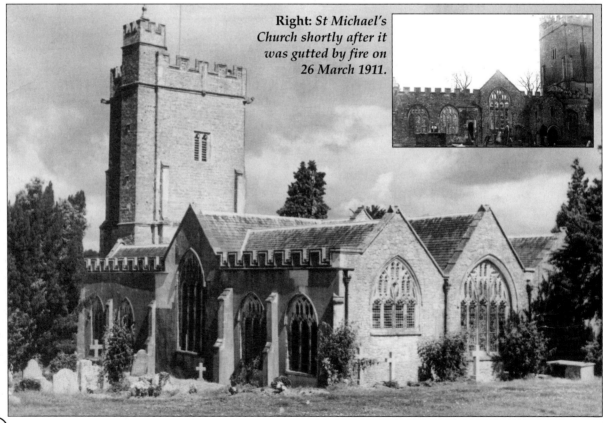

Right: *St Michael's Church shortly after it was gutted by fire on 26 March 1911.*

of 11 bays, 48 feet in length, had a crossing nave and aisles, three pairs of gates with the vaulting and cornices intact on both sides. The vaulting supported a loft 6 feet wide. Each fan consisted of six panels with richly embossed tracery. Above the vaulting was an exquisitely carved cornice, exhibiting the usual vine-leaf ornament. It was of exceptional merit, both the excellence of the carving and its perfect condition. It was an irreparable loss, fire doing what the Henrican iconoclasts had failed to do. The remains of the stone stairway that led to the rood-loft can be seen in the wall of the north aisle. The church was quickly rebuilt, and within a year it was reopened. Sadly, again, a single beam replaced the rood-screen. Chairs, which never really look right in a church, took the place of the pews.

Dr Peter Courtenay, both Bishop of Exeter and lord of the manor of Honiton, built the tower and nave towards the end of the fifteenth century, the chancel being rebuilt at the start of the sixteenth century by Henry Takell. The tower was built with local Buckerell stone and contains six bells. The oldest is the third bell (1719), the second and the tenor arriving in 1749; both were cast by the well-known Thomas Bilbie of Cullompton. The treble dates from 1901, the same time that the bells were rehung by Henry Stokes of Woodbury.

Inside, the tomb of Thomas Marwood, one of Honiton's most famous sons who lived at Marwood House, can be seen to the left of the north wall. The inscription reads:

Here lieth the body of Thomas Marwood. Gent: who practised Physick and Chirurgery, above 75 years, and being zealous of good works, gave certain Houses and bequeathed in his will to the Poor of Honiton, 10 pounds and being aged above 105 years departed in the Catholic Faith, September ye 18th Anno Domini 1617.

There is a story often told that the good people of Honiton wanted to build a church in the centre of their town but the 'Devil' was against the idea. The stones for the church were carried into the town every day and every night Satan carried them to the top of the hill. After a while the people got tired carrying the same stones down the hill and decided to build St Michael's on the spot that the Devil obviously wanted. Apocalyptic? Maybe, but why else would anyone build a church half a mile away and up a steep hill?

Rookwood Rectory

Rookwood Rectory, the old rectory in Honiton, was demolished in the late 1970s and redeveloped as housing and flats. A new rectory was built close to the site of the former one. In the 1960s the late Alice Bambury put on paper what she remembered of the old building during Revd Frederick Leslie Courtenay's rectorship. He was rector of Honiton

between 1908–35, becoming the 16th Earl of Devon on the death of his older brother.

My memories of Rookwood take me back over half a century when the Revd Frederick Courtenay, his wife and six children lived there.

At that time Mrs Marguerite started the Girls Friendly Society in Honiton and kindly allowed the meetings to be held in Rookwood's large dining-room. The number of girls who joined the Society, of whom I was one, was about 20.

There was little for young people to do in Honiton at that time. No radio, television, library or playing-fields, so we greatly looked forward to our meetings of the G.F.S.

Mrs Courtenay, who was a kind motherly lady, presided. We had Bible readings and talks on various subjects of interest to girls of our age. In the winter the second half of the meeting was given over to indoor games such as chess, dominoes and draughts. In the summer we played in the lovely Rookwood gardens. We climbed trees, played hide and seek and rounders. We then took turns to feed the huge lazy tortoise with dandelions.

When the rector's five daughters were home they amused us by acting charades, dressing up in the wonderful old clothes, which were kept in an old chest.

The rector usually paid us a visit during our meetings. He was a large jovial gentleman of whom we were really rather in awe. He was invariably wearing his clerical dress, which consisted of a black coat and waistcoat, knee breeches, long stockings and black shoes with large silver buckles on the toes. We all treated him with great respect.

During this time, in the very early 1920s, a very grand pageant was produced in Honiton called 'Children Through The Centuries'. Many of the town's organisations such as the Sunday schools, Rangers, Guides, Brownies and Children's Union took part, each producing their own tableau. The rector's tableau, in which I took part, was entitled 'Child Marriages'. It was a medieval scene, and we spared no effort to get the costumes that were authentic to the period.

The pageant was staged in the Mackarness Hall. No form of entertainment was allowed in St Paul's Church, only conventional church services being allowed there. It was a sad parting when the rector had to leave Rookwood House in order to take up residence in

Marwood House, High Street, c.1930.

Powderham Castle. This, I think, took place in the mid 1930s, when the rector succeeded his older brother as the Earl of Devon. Unfortunately the rector did not live long after leaving Honiton. His only son, Christopher, has now succeeded him to the Earldom.

Last Friday I passed Rookwood and was very sad and nostalgic when I saw the large open space where Rookwood House had stood for so many years.

The Roman Catholic Church of the Holy Family

The establishment of the Church of England during the reign of Henry VIII (1509–47) stemmed not from any dislike of the Roman Catholic Church but from the fact that Pope Clement refused to grant Henry papal dispensation to divorce Catherine of Aragon and marry Anne Boleyn. Henry hoped to solve his problem by citing the Law of Praemunire in 1531 stating that the whole church was guilty of treason, but allowing the clergy to buy pardons if they would recognise him as supreme head of the Church in England. By offering the clergy pardons Henry gambled on the Pope granting him his divorce, but the ruse failed. What followed is history. Henry became the supreme head of the Church in England, but became the Church of England rather than the Roman Catholic Church.

For many years the Catholic Church was persecuted, but not enough to prevent Thomas Marwood from being buried at St Michael's in 1617 and having the words 'departed in the Catholic Faith' inscribed on his tomb. However, active Catholicism did not return to the Honiton area until 1877 when the Hon. Colin and Lady Frances Lindsay successfully sought the Pope's permission to have a family chaplain at their Deer Park House. It was there that what is thought to have been the first mass to be said in the area for over 300 years since the Reformation took place.

A year later an outhouse was converted into a chapel and masses were said on and off until 1898, when the acquisition of a plot of land on Church Hill saw the arrival of the 'Iron Church', a gift of the Duke of Norfolk (the Howards are a leading Catholic family in England). It was transported from Sussex and re-erected in Honiton and the altar, stained glass and furniture from Deer Park were also brought there and incorporated in the new building. A house was bought in New Street to serve as a presbytery – it still stands just below the railway bridge at the time of writing.

The next milestone in a growing church's history was the establishment of Honiton as a parish in its own right in 1927 by Bishop John Kelly, and the first parish priest was Revd William Fox.

A growing church brought a problem with it; the Iron Church, which was also deteriorating, was not now big enough to hold its congregation. For a time a temporary home was found at Broomhills, until 1937, and the Church of the Holy Family on the Exeter Road next to Broomhills, now St Rita's College and a Recollect Seminary for young students to the priesthood, was built.

The church is a handsome building in the Gothic style and constructed with golden-brown facing bricks. Inside there are four gothic-style windows on each side of the nave. The Lindsay Memorial Chapel is a memorial to the Hon. Colin and Lady Frances Lindsay and it has on it the arms of the Crawford and Wicklow families. The altar in the chapel is the original one from Deer Park (the Lindsay's country home) and the main altar has a panel of Ashburton marble.

Methodist Chapel

The Methodist Chapel was in New Street but it was closed in around the late 1970s, probably on financial grounds, and purchased by the local council. It was then used as a Senior Citizen's Centre and also houses the town clerk's office and the council chamber. The Methodists then held their meetings in the Wesley Hall in Chapel Street, which had formerly been a Sunday school and also a venue for parties and concerts.

In his story of the Honiton of his youth (c.1913) Edgar William Pulman amusingly said that he attended this Sunday school because they gave better Sunday school treats and outings than St Paul's Church.

Dunkeswell Abbey

Dunkeswell Abbey lies some 6 miles to the north of Honiton on the tiny Madford River that flows away to the north to join the River Culm, where it then finds a wider life in the English Channel via the River Exe. It is located at the right-hand turning at the top of the village, where the road to Hemyock makes a right-angled left turn before reaching the airfield.

This is typical Blackdown country. Rolling hills (the airfield is 688 feet above sea level) with plenty of trees, and farms standing at the end of long lanes in the same places as those at the time of Domesday. There is reference to Stentwood Farm, almost on the abbey's doorstep, from as early as the twelfth century

Indeed the abbey itself is almost as old, being first built in wood in 1201 by 12 monks who had walked there from Forde Abbey near Chard in Somerset. Lord William Brewer, who gave the abbey to the Cistercian order, his wife Beatrice, John, the Abbot of Forde, and the Abbot of the Cistercian mother abbey in England at Waverley watched the opening ceremony. Lord Brewer was an important man in England at the turn of the twelfth century and a friend of Richard I (1189–99) for whom he acted as proxy during his absence at the

Wolford Chapel, c.1995.

The Bishop's Tower, Honiton, in c.1918.

Crusades. Five years after the first wooden building was erected King John confirmed its foundation.

There is an abstract of Lord Brewer's original charter in the records of the Duchy of Lancaster:

To all Christ's faithful to whom the present deed shall come. William Brewer, greeting. Know all of you that I, for the salvation of my Lords Henry and Richard, Kings of England, and the souls of my father and mother, and my soul and those of Beatrice, my wife. And my children and all my ancestors and successors, have given and granted to God and Blessed Mary and the Cistercian order all my lands of Donkewell and of Wolfchurche, with the advowsons of the churches of the aforesaid lands, and all their appurtenances, in free, pure and personal alms, quit of all services and secular exactions, to build an Abbey of the aforesaid Order from the Convent of Forde. And that my gift and grant may remain firm forever I have corroborated it with the present deed and appending of my seal.

William Brewer was buried at Dunkeswell in 1226 and, in order be buried there, he gave up all his possessions in the presence of Henry III (1216–72) at Westminster and became a lay-brother at the abbey. Beatrice, his wife, was also buried there although her remains were later re-interred in the grounds when the new church was built in 1842 by Elizabeth Posthuma Simcoe, the wife of General Simcoe, the first Governor General of Upper Canada (now the province of Ontario), who claimed descent from William Brewer – her second burial spot is marked by a tree.

Like so many splendid abbeys and monasteries Dunkeswell was ransacked by Henry VIII's men at the time of the Dissolution in 1539. The abbey was left to moulder away, a process that was exacerbated by many local farmers who helped themselves to much of the stonework. All that remains in 2005 are the former gatehouse and piles of stone that mark the spot of the cloister.

Wolford Chapel

The Simcoe connection can be found nearer Honiton at Wolford, part of the Simcoe estate, where the Blackdown Hills begin their descent to the River Otter and Honiton. It was there in 1802 that General John Graves Simcoe built Wolford Chapel on the ruins of what is said to have been a medieval abbey, a site approximately 88 feet by 65 feet.

In 1966 the publisher Sir Geoffrey Harmsworth donated the chapel to the people of Ontario. At that time Mr A. Le Marchant, then owner of the Simcoe estate, donated an easement as a right of way. The Ontario Heritage Foundation in trust has owned the chapel for the people of Ontario since 1982. Signposts to the chapel are marked with the Canadian flag and the flag is flown outside the chapel.

There is a plaque in memory of the General, his wife, and their five daughters, who are all buried around the chapel building.

The Bishop's Tower

Just off the A35 to the east of Honiton stands the Bishop's Tower that was erected by Edward Copleston, Bishop of Llandaff and Dean of St Paul's, who also built the stone pump head at the crossroads in the middle of Offwell. The pump head is located on the probable spot of the well from which Offwell, 'Offa's weille', takes it name. Bishop Copleston built Offwell House (the Rectory in 1845) as well as the tower on Honiton Hill, the Bishop's Tower, of course. He was said to have been able to enjoy some magnificent views of Honiton and the Otter valley from there including, on a fine day, over the Blackdown Hills and into his Llandaff bishopric. Actually, he would have needed around another 100 feet to do that. The Copleston family provided seven successive vicars of Offwell between 1773 and 1965. The incumbent there in 1900 was Revd J.H.H. Copleston, later curate at Kilmington and a cricketer of considerable ability with both bat

Looking down at Honiton from the fields on the west side of Church Hill in 1960. At the front to the left is part of Honiton Hospital.

Left: *Honiton's old Marlpits Hospital from the rear in 1992; the photographer was standing on the site of the new hospital.*

The old Marlpits Hospital and former workhouse on 11 March 1992.

Above: *Honiton's new telephone exchange in 1984.*

Left: *Honiton's new hospital during its construction in 1994.*

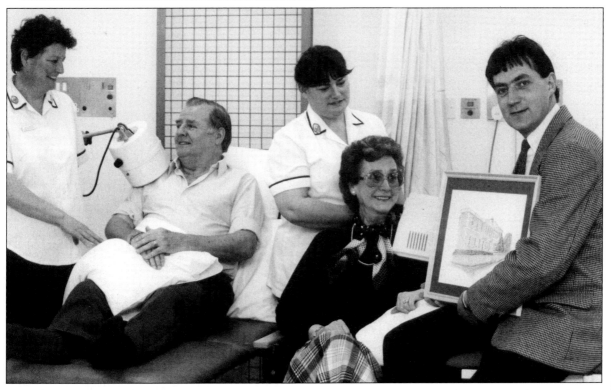

The first patients at the new Honiton Hospital physiotherapy department on 20 February 1995. Left to right: Liz Proctor (senior physiotherapist), Roy Bright (first male patient), Lynne Smith (superintendent physiotherapist), Isabel Nobbs (first female patient), Patrick McDonagh (locality manager).

and ball. His main clubs were Seaton and Kilmington but he turned out for most local clubs including Honiton. It is said that he arranged his funerals to fit in with his cricket rather than the other way around, and he played cricket six days a week. It was also claimed that he had thought up a way of getting a game on Sundays but never found the courage to float it past the Bishop of Exeter.

During the Second World War the local Home Guard used the tower as a lookout post.

The Workhouse and Hospital

The Workhouse, or the Honiton Union to give its proper name, was founded after the passing of the Poor Law Amendment Act of 1834. The Revd B. Lewis, the chairman of the Governors' Building Committee, laid the building's foundation-stone on 5 October 1836. The grim and austere building in Marlpit Lane looked out over the town from above the railway station for the next 160 years, until it was replaced with the modern hospital in 1996. It had plenty of custom – a newspaper report stated that '155 paupers had been treated to a Christmas Day [1841] meal of roast beef and plum pudding.' At a time when the population of the town was around 3,750 there were as many as 155 in the workhouse, and probably more because some would have been too sick to eat such rich food and others were probably serving a term of punishment. And that is not even considering the number of people outside the workhouse who were threshold cases for admittance.

Laws governing the provision of relief for the poor in England had existed for at least four centuries before the opening of the Honiton Union. In 1536 an act for the relief of the 'impotent poor' was passed. Even so, beggars in good health were expected to work and the cost of maintaining those who could not was met from voluntary subscriptions, and the parish carried out the administration.

Honiton's old parish workhouse was built in 1738 in what is now New Street on the site of what became Summerland Place. After the building of the new workhouse in Marlpit Lane it was knocked down in 1839.

Such parishes tried their hardest to wriggle out from their responsibilities, parish registers often referring to beggars or other 'n'ere do wells' being 'escorted to the parish boundary'. No doubt they were sent on their way with a well-aimed kick and threats as to what might happen if they returned.

Closer to home, in 1769 a servant died in a house, but, being a pauper, his funeral was chargeable to the parish. The problem was that the house and its outbuildings lay in the parishes of Colyton, Farway and Southleigh. Colyton soon wriggled out of any payment, stating that the only buildings actually in its parish was a dairy. But the boundary between Southleigh and Farway ran through the room in which the man had died. King Solomon would have been proud of these men; they next decided that the criterion had to be the parish in which his head was resting when he died – and Farway ended up with the bill.

The Poor Laws were amended from time to time. In 1601 a Poor Law Act imposed a rate for poor relief on property owners and in 1662 an Act of Settlement was passed that gave local overseers the right to return to their parish of birth any person not from their parish who owed no land there and was unemployed.

The 1723 Workhouse Test Act forced people in receipt of relief to enter a workhouse, this being amended by the 1834 Act (the Speenhamland System) that gave rise to Honiton's workhouse and saw the withdrawal of all outdoor relief. This forced the poor into workhouses in which 'the conditions were unpleasant by design'. By 1905 a Royal Commission on the Poor Laws was appointed. As is the way with Royal Commissions, it was in no hurry, taking until 1909 to report its findings. They did not really support the recommendations of one member, Beatrice Webb, a Fabian, who wanted to go much further than that age and generation was prepared to go. But 'times were a changing'. Lloyd George's Old Age Pensions had been introduced in 1908 and his National Insurance Act followed in 1910. At the end of the Second World War Winston Churchill's Conservative Government introduced family allowances and the National Health Service was born a few years later. The age of the workhouse was over and at Honiton it became the town's hospital.

From time to time one reads that life in the workhouse was not as bad as it was made out to be. Just possibly it was not so bad at Christmas and other festive occasions such as royal coronations and jubilees or the ending of wars. For the rest of the year in Honiton the inmates, which is what they were officially (and cruelly) called, led a drab, dreary and ill-treated existence. Honiton inmates were expected to wear a badge on their clothes – you were not only poor, but the authorities wanted everyone to know that you were.

Apart from at the festive occasions the inmates' dreary existence was usually kept well away from the outside world. But the better days, or rather the munificence of those who donated towards them, received much coverage in the local press. The day of 7 January 1908 was typical example at which the mayor and mayoress (Alderman and Mrs Harry Banfield) entertained the inmates at Honiton Workhouse to a great treat that included entertainment by Harry Rice of Exeter. The great event was held in the dining-hall, which was decorated with garlands of evergreens, pictures and paper decorations – a bright and cheerful scene. The decorations had been the work of Mr and Mrs Key (the master and matron) 'who ruled those

The opening of the Jerrard Wing extension in 1957. Pictured are, left to right: ?, ?, Mr W. Board (mayor), Mr Dunning, Mrs Phillips, Mrs Haw (behind), the matron (name unknown).

Above: *Honiton town crier Joe Lake being 'stretchered' into the new hospital on 21 March 1996, the day after the new baby unit was opened.*

Right: *Audrey Hayman* (left), *an auxiliary nurse at Marlpits Hospital since 1965, cuts the first turf on the new hospital site on 20 September 1993. Sylvia Russell lends a helping hand.*

grimy halls'. Other officials had helped them, but it is hard not to suspect that 'volunteers' from among the inmates had done the heavy work.

As many as 70 inmates sat down, and the presence of the mayor and mayoress, the chaplain, Revd R. Seymour, Mrs Seymour and two of the guardians, Mr Creber and Mr J. Broom, went a long way towards ensuring the absence of that fine old English ballad 'It was Christmas Day in the Workhouse, the Day of all the Year' from the lengthy repertoire that Harry Rice gave. It included songs, tales and conjuring tricks. The songs were loudly applauded and his tales in the Devonshire dialect caused roars of laughter. His 'exceedingly clever and smartly performed conjuring tricks baffled everyone and his ventriloqial [sic] dialogue was much admired.' He was truly a man of many skills. During the interval, sandwiches, buns, coffee and cigarettes were handed around, the food having been provided by the mayor and mayoress who were warmly thanked at the end of the evening by the chaplain. The hearty three cheers that followed were proof that the inmates had much enjoyed and appreciated the food – or so said the chaplain; no record remains that anyone so lowly as an inmate was actually allowed to get up and say

thank you. Perhaps authority was frightened of what he or she might say. It was a harsh age after all. At the nearby Axminster Workhouse a woman had recently been sentenced to 14 days' hard labour by the Axminster magistrates for refusing to do the washing up.

The National Health Act of 1948 gave the Honiton Union the status of a hospital. It still looked grim outside but inside it was becoming welcoming and homely, a process hastened by the building of the Jerrard Wing in 1957, now used for the long-stay patients. An attractive sun lounge was added in around 1962 but campaigners were already crying out for a brand-new building. They had to wait 30 years until 1996 when the new building was finally opened. Construction work started in 1993, the 33-bed hospital was estimated to cost just over £4,000,000.

In 1997 the hospital acquired teaching status for the first time when it was linked by satellite to Plymouth University. This meant that trainee nurses not only received practical experience in the wards but the also received lectures and academic trading via computers set up in the Jerrard Wing – the only remaining part of the old building.

Marlpits Hospital shortly before its demolition.

Above: *In around 1960 the Honiton branch of the Royal British Legion presented a seat to the local hospital in memory of Miss Dunning. The picture includes: Dr Catherine Glanvill, Margaret Robson, Linda Were, Mrs Stamp, Mrs Hurford, Mr Farragher (at back), Mrs Summers, Mr Dunning, Queenie Tozer, Mrs Morgan, Reg Gigg, Dr Terry Glanvill, Mrs Millard (in front), Mrs Ridler, Bill Strawbridge.*

Left: *Alf Taylor outside Marlpits Hospital, where he worked as a porter, on 30 March 1995.*

Chapter 11

Honiton Show and Fair

SHOW PRESIDENTS

1890 Rt Hon. Viscount Sidmouth	1958 Robert Williams Esq.
1891 Sir John Kennaway Bt MP	1959 F.E. Pyle Esq.
1892 Richard Marker Esq.	1960 Mary Viscountess Sidmouth
1893 Rt Hon. Earl Compton MP	1961 E.C.W. Tuke Esq.
1894 C.D. Cave Esq.	1962 R.A. Merrick Esq.
1895 W. Edmonds Esq. JP	1963 Commander G.C. Boles RN
1896 D.W.R. Buchanan Esq.	1964 Lt Col R.F.P. Eames
1897 Major J.E.H. Balfour	1965 Major W. Halswell
1898 Lord Coleridge QC	1966 Major W. Halswell
1899 Sir John Kennaway Bt MP	1967 B.M. Lindsay Fynn Esq.
1900 Richard Marker Esq.	1968 Austen Reynolds Esq.
1901 Revd W.H. White	1969 Austen Reynolds Esq.
1902–13 No records available	1970 J.N. Welch-Thornton Esq.
1914–18 First World War	1971 Sir Charles Cave Bt
1919 Willoughby S. Smith Esq. MFH	1972 O.N.W. William-Powlett Esq.
1920 Sir John Kennaway Bt JP	1973 J.F.C. Dugdale Esq.
1921 Sir John Kennaway Bt JP	1974 J.R. McKeig-Jones Esq.
1922 Major A.C. Morrison Bell MP	1975 Dr A.T.H. Glanvill
1923 Colonel J.E.H. Balfour CMG DSO	1976 Major C.R.C. Elverson
1924 Willoughby S. Smith Esq. MFH	1977 Right Hon. Peter Emery MP
1925 Sir Charles Cave Bt JP	1978 Sir Peter Watkins Williams
1926 Major E.G. Weldon JP	1979 E.R. Lawrence Esq.
1927 Harley Granville-Barker Esq.	1980 E.J. Goddard Esq.
1928 Major Gen. Sir Harold Tagart KMOG CB DSO	1981 F.L. Turl Esq.
1929 J.R. Makeig-Jones Esq.	1982 Lord Clinton JP DL
1930 Colonel L.C. Garrett OBE	1983 W. Angus Murray Esq.
1931 Colonel A.D. Acland CBE TD JP	1984 M. Holland-Hibbert DL Esq.
1932 Colonel A.D. Acland CBE TD JP	1985 Dame Elizabeth Butler-Sloss DBE
1933 Revd the Hon. L.L. Courtenay	1986 G.O.C. Allhusen Esq.
1934 Captain John L. Hunter	1987 P. Luscombe Esq. JP
1935 Captain P.G.R. Benson	1988 G.H. Twitt Esq.
1936 W.E.B. Copland-Crawford Esq.	1989 Sir Jack Boles MBE DL
1937 Sir Edward C. Cave	1990 Rear Ad. Sir Ronald Forrest KCVO JP DL
1938 R.R.K. Marker JP Esq.	1991 G.L.G. Noel Esq.
1939 Major E.F. Talbot-Ponsonby MFH	1992 A.J. Luxton Esq.
1940–45 Second World War	1993 Bryan A. Harris Esq.
1946 Sir John Kennaway Bt DL JP	1994 Edward Disney Esq.
1947 Major B.N. William-Powlett	1995 Major General Sir John Acland KCB CBE DL
1948 E.R. Marker Esq.	1996 Richard J.T. Marker Esq.
1949 Henry Hopkinson Esq. CMG	1997 Richard J.T. Marker Esq.
1950 Dr R.N. Craig MFH	1998 Malcolm Floey Esq.
1951 Brigadier P.B.E. Acland OBE MC	1999 N.F.A. Page-Turner Esq. DL
1952 Sir John Kennaway Bt DL JP	2000 Richard J.T. Marker Esq.
1953 Brigadier E.L. Griffith-Williams CBE DSO MC	2001 Dr C.M. Davidson
1954 J.N. Welch-Thornton Esq.	2002 Angela Browning MP
1955 Captain N.J.W. William DSC RN	2003 Anthony Gibson OBE
1956 Col Sir Edmond Schreiber	2004 General Sir John Waters GCB CBE DL JP
1957 Major General Roland Denning KCB DSO DL CB MVO DL	2005 F.E. Martin

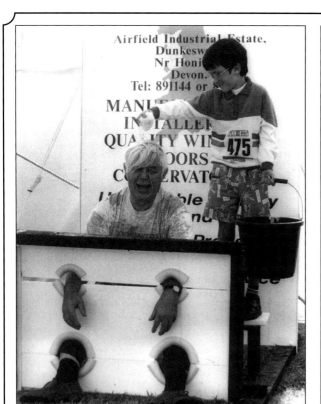

Dunkeswell man Dave Crompton, who spent the day in the stocks at the 1992 Honiton Show, is seen getting yet another soaking.

The cattle judge, Mr Tom Emm, presents the Supreme Show Champion to Chillaton Cornets Alicia, a Jersey cow owned by Mr John Taylor of Palm Hill.

Right: The presentation to Frank Pyle on the occasion of his retirement as Honiton Show secretary in 1963 after 43 years' service. Pictured are, left to right: ?, Edwin Martin (chairman), Commander G.C. Boles (president), Frank Pyle, Jack Luxton (secretary).

PC Atyeo and a colleague move the stallholders on from Honiton High Street in December 1992.

Honiton Show

The Honiton Agricultural Association Show, to give it its proper name, but hereinafter called Honiton Show, which is what everyone calls it, was born in 1890 when the Awliscombe, Buckerell, Feniton and Gittisham Agricultural Association felt that there was a need to hold a show. A meeting was held at the Dolphin Hotel when the decision to include Honiton in the association and go ahead with the show was made. This led to the association being renamed as the Honiton and District Store Cattle, Poultry, Butter and Cream Association. In that humble way was born what is now probably the biggest and best one-day agricultural event in the country.

The first show was held at Bramble Hill on 30 September 1890 when the admission charge was one shilling (5p). Among the prizes was one of five guineas (£5.25p) for the best Devon bull in the show, as well as prizes of £1.10.0d. (£1.50p) and 15 shillings (75p) for the best pigs.

Lord Sidmouth accepted an invitation to be the show's first president and even then there was sufficient work to be done that three joint secretaries, H. Banfield, E.W. Hellier and John Hussey, were appointed. That first show attracted not only a large crowd, but also considerable interest – so much so that a William Skinner of Escot Lane, Ottery St Mary, composed a poem that was discovered in his notebook many years later by his granddaughter, Mary Skinner of Taleford, near Escot. It may not be of Poet Laureate quality but it is certainly worth a place in this chapter:

Ode to Honiton Show

Oh what a day we're having I'm sure,
For the Honiton people both rich and poor,
Have made up their minds to have a spree,

Honiton Show treasurer Edwin Martin leads the procession of 'Farm Transport Through The Ages' into the ring at the 1989 show. (PICTURE BY KIND PERMISSION OF MR J.M. OAKLEY)

And the Agricultural Show to see.
The town is all alive today,
With thousands of people from far away,
And triumphal arches decked with green,
Made Honiton look like a fairy scene.
Flags and banners are everywhere,
And snobs and tailors I do declare,
To keep up their spirits while at the show,
They'll get jolly well boozy before they go.
There is country chaps come from the plough,
And carroty Nance that milks the cow,
And pot-bellied farmers all of a row,
Will come many miles to see the show.
There is Johnny, Billy, Harry and Bob,
And knock-kneed Sal with a woolly bob,
Who must mend her stocking before she's wed.
Here's the Viscount of Sidmouth jolly good health,
May he long live to enjoy good health,
Likewise his stewards and tenants as well,
They are regular trumps the truth I will tell.
In the show yard you will see the machine there at work,
Tearing away like the Russians and Turk,
And the Royal Marine Band from church will go,
And play you sweet music right up to the show.
There are pretty girls and lots of prizes,
And you may be sure all sorts of surprises,
Machines for grinding old women's knees,
And for making the Babies' teas.
From Exeter, Broadclyst and Pinhoe,
And from Whimple they are sure to go,
And the Ottery girls and chaps will go

Skipping along to see the show.
There's simple Johnny and flashy Jane,
Who they say is the dandy of Spillers Lane.
There are several others who come you know,
Enjoying a day at Honiton Show.
The bells will ring and the band will play,
Let everybody shout 'Hooray',
The girls of Honiton with their pretty face,
Are going to show a waggon [sic] of lace,
Chorus. So drink to success before you go,
To the Devonshire Agricultural Show.

Known by then as the Honiton Union Agricultural Association's Show, Honiton Show was not held during the First World War but it was restarted following a public meeting at the Dolphin Hotel on 27 March 1920, at which Sir John Kennaway accepted an invitation to be president. He followed in the footsteps of his late father, also Sir John Kennaway, and Honiton's MP for 40 years. Reg Cruwys and Frank Pyle were elected as joint secretaries. The association had £78 invested in War Loan Stock at the time. A committee of as many as 50 people was elected and it included Lord Sidmouth and an appropriately named Mr Farmer from Ottery St Mary. In 1932 the show's territory was enlarged to include all of the Honiton

Honiton Show, 1912.

Right, below and bottom: *Honiton Show at the Heathfield site in the late 1920s.*

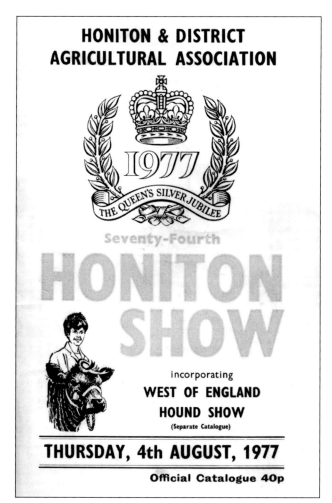

HONITON & DISTRICT AGRICULTURAL ASSOCIATION

1977

THE QUEEN'S SILVER JUBILEE

Seventy-Fourth

HONITON SHOW

incorporating
WEST OF ENGLAND HOUND SHOW
(Separate Catalogue)

THURSDAY, 4th AUGUST, 1977

Official Catalogue 40p

Mr Stevens of Halberton with his heavy horses that won a first prize in their class at the 1988 Honiton Show.

The Centenary Show (1990) was a huge success, attracting around 30,000 people. They saw a sure sign of Honiton Show's continually rising status by its selection to host the British Saanens regional breed finals in the goat section that year.

Honiton Fair

There has been a fair in Honiton since 1221 when it was granted by Henry III. Originally the fair was held on the 'eve day and morrow of Allhallows'. At the time of writing it is held on the Wednesday and Thursday following 19 July. The entry in Pipe Roll, 5 Hen III, concerning the 1221 fair stated that 'Falkes de Breautee owed a palfrey for having a yearly fair at the manor of Honeton on eve day and morrow off All Hallows.' The same Falkes de Breautee is said in the Testa Nevil for 1217–21, to 'hold the borough of Huneton by reason of his wardship of Baldwin de Redvers by grant of our lord the King and it is worth four marks.' Baldwin de Redvers was a minor who had become the Seventh Earl of Devon on the death of his grandfather, William de Redvers, in 1217.

Until modern times the fair was held in the High Street which was full of stalls offering local produce and cheapjack wares. There was a brisk horse sale as well. The dictates of modern traffic drove the fair into a field on the Exeter road, where merry-go-rounds, bearded ladies, boxing booths and other amusements filled the vacuum caused by the diminished trade in livestock. In the 1950s the fair was held in the Fair Field.

The former Samuel Manley, woodsman for Lord Sidmouth at Upottery who visited every fair for over 60 years, used to tell many a story of bygone fairs:

When I was a boy [1870] we used to come in from the outlying villages and lodge in the public houses, when they kept open day and night, and make a week of it. There were many fights between the rival gypsies whose favourite meeting place was the Red Cow. Before the fair moved to the Fair Field, the merry-go-rounds, shooting galleries and gingerbread stalls were in the High Street

Parliamentary Division, with the exception of the Axminster Union District. Axminster had previously held a show and was considering reviving it (although it never did). In 1935 the Whimple area was included as well.

Frank Pyle would remain in office as secretary for 43 years and was also president in 1959. At the time of writing four of the last six MPs to represent Honiton have been presidents of the show – Sir John Kennaway, Major Clive Morrison Bell, Peter Emery and Angela Browning. Robert Matthew was probably not the member for Honiton long enough but the exclusion of Sir Cedric Drewe is certainly a surprise. There have been three women presidents – the first being Mary Viscountess Sidmouth who, in 1960, ended 70 years of (unintended) male chauvinism.

Like Topsy, Honiton Show 'just grow'd', soon outgrowing its first home at Bramble Hill. In May 1921 an offer of use of the old Camp Ground just outside Honiton was accepted. After the end of the Second World War the show had to look for a new home and it moved to the foot of Ottery Moor Lane, where both the cricket and football clubs are housed at the time of writing. From there a move was made to the Monkton Road ground and, in time for the 2003 show, another move saw the show housed in what looks like being a permanent home at Roebuck Farm.

Above: *Alison Salter, Tina Welch, and Carole Urquhart in charge of the Busy Bee Crèche at the 1992 Honiton Show.*

Left: *Dental hygienist Ann Van Der Gaaun of Honiton, with the help of Horace, the horse, shows six-year-old Jamie Perryman from Whimple how to brush his teeth properly at the 1994 Honiton Show.*

Right: *The 1988 Honiton Show's Horse and Hound Show.*

Below: *Mrs Rae of Tedburn St Mary and her Shetland-pony-driven carriage was a great attraction at the 1988 Honiton Show.*

Tich Hammett from Shute, near Honiton, with his animal that won the Breed Championship for Rouge De L'ouest sheep at the 1992 Honiton Show.

The 1992 Honiton Show Supreme Beef Champion, shown here by Colin Hutchings, stockman to the owner, Fran Evens.

A 1980 flower show with, left to right, Mr Heapy, Richard Pike, Margaret Robson and Louisa Heapy admiring the sweet peas.

Members of the Honiton and the Feniton Girl Guides act as messengers at the 1991 Honiton Show.

Honiton Show in 1988.

Honiton Hill Rally in 1990.

and Anderton & Rowlands held their funfair there, Brewers' had their three-abreast galloping horses in the Lamb Inn's yard, Hancock's amusements were in the top field and there was a circus in the lower field.

Fair Day was also regarded as 'pay day', farmers coming in to pay their yearly or half-yearly bills. The tradesmen entertained their customers to dinner and their wives and children to tea. One tradesman said that he provided 120 pounds of beef and an 18-gallon cask of beer on Fair Day for his customers, some of whom, after partaking of his hospitality, would forget to pay their bills.

On the day before the fair the town crier, in his braided coat and cocked hat, moves up the High Street to the Market House where, at noon, he shouts out the traditional words that officially open the fair:

Oyez! Oyez! Oyez! The Glove is up! The Glove is up! The Glove is up! The Fair is begun! The Fair is begun! The Fair is begun! No man shall be arrested! No man shall be arrested! No man shall be arrested! Until the Glove is taken down! Until the Glove is taken down! Until the Glove is taken down! God Save the Queen!

The origins of these words are lost in the mists of time but it is generally accepted that they have not been altered for a very long time, and were the signal for fights to break out as family feuds were settled (or resettled). The meaning of the extended glove may

have also been lost in the passing of time, but it is possible that it was originally intended to be a symbol of freedom from imprisonment for debtors who were thrown into jail if caught by their creditors. The open hand is recognised as symbolising friendship and immunity from being arrested during the three days of the fair – but only for debtors. The Glove and the Pole was attached to the front of the King's Arms for the duration of the Cattle Fair which was held in the street outside the hotel. On the Thursday they were then taken down High Street to the White Lion and placed there for the duration of the Horse Fair. After 1975, when the King's Arms closed, the glove was hoisted outside the Angel.

Almost certainly the Horse Fair was held outside the White Lion because of its closeness to the fairly steep climb from the Gissage up to the Globe, up which would-be horse purchasers would watch the horses being 'run' to prove them to be of sound wind and limb. It was harder work at nearby Axminster. There the horses were sold at the top of Castle Hill, over twice as long and steep as the 'run' in Honiton.

A curious feature of the opening day of the fair is the throwing of hot pennies from the upper windows of the Angel Hotel (until it closed), the White Lion and the New Dolphin. The custom is said to have originated as a cheap joke when local gentry gathered at the inns and laughed as the children tried to pick up the almost red-hot coins. Today they are nowhere near as hot.

Above: Children (mostly boys) scramble for hot pennies on a Honiton Fair Day, c.1912.

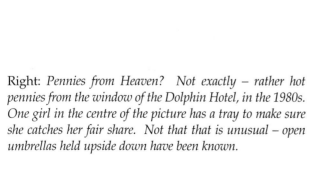

Right: Pennies from Heaven? Not exactly – rather hot pennies from the window of the Dolphin Hotel, in the 1980s. One girl in the centre of the picture has a tray to make sure she catches her fair share. Not that that is unusual – open umbrellas held upside down have been known.

Above: *Honiton children scrambling for the hot pennies in 1890 – they would have been harder to find among the stones of the unpaved High Street at the time.*

Right: *Honiton's High Street decorated for Honiton Show on 22 May 1879. The horse-chestnut tree is still there at the time of writing.*

Children waiting outside the Angel Hotel in the 1930s for the hot pennies to be thrown from the upstairs window.

Seen here in around 1912, steam engines such as this powered the stalls or amusements owned by Messrs Anderton & Rowlands and were used at Honiton Fair.

Donald Thomas with 'Jubilee' at the 1994 Honiton Hill Rally.

Honitonians seen in their Sunday best at an Edwardian Honiton Fair.

Right: *Some of the crowds that flocked to the 1993 Honiton Show.*

Below: *The town crier Joe Lake at the 1988 hot pennies ceremony; on his left is the mayor, Robert Walker, and a previous mayor, Dr Terry Glanvill.*

Below: *The mayor, Dr Terry Glanvill (second from the right), and the town crier, Joe Lake (far right), head the procession up High Street for the hot pennies ceremony in the 1980s. But where are the town crier's pole and glove? Mr Heapy is to the left of Dr Glanvill, Walt Summers, a former mayor (in a white shirt), is behind him.*

Chapter 12
Roads and Railways

For many years the heavy summer traffic heading for the sea, sand and sunshine of Devon and Cornwall made life a misery for both driver and pedestrian alike as it queued along the A30, especially on Saturdays, to enter Honiton from both directions. The problem was exacerbated by the traffic down the hill on the now A35 from Axminster that was trying to filter into the main street. It often took over half an hour to travel from one end of the town to the other and pedestrians often took their lives in their hands when they tried to cross the road. All that was ended in 1966 when the then Minister of Transport, Barbara Castle, officially opened the new bypass that ran towards Exeter almost as far as Fenny Bridges. The bypass cost £900,000 to construct and, during the excavation work prehistoric remains, including the bones of two elephants and of giant oxen, red deer and a hippopotamus, were discovered some 15 feet below the surface.

Work on the bypass began on 24 July 1964, immediately after Lord Chesham, Joint Parliamentary Secretary to the then Minister of Transport, Ernest Marples, 'cut the first sod' with a massive D8 Caterpillar and scraper. The bypass involved around 300,000 cubic yards of earthworks and it was estimated that there would be an equal ration of 'cut' to 'fill'. It was 2.1 miles in length but has since (1998–99) become part of the new A30 dual carriageway that stretches from Monkton to the east of Honiton as far as Exeter. It gained notoriety in both the press and on TV as 'the noisiest road in Britain'.

The *Express & Echo* said that 'the need for a bypass had first been raised over twenty years earlier.' But, in fact, the question of a bypass was certainly mooted as early as 1938 when the Honiton Chamber of Commerce was formed under the presidency of local solicitor Mr T. Phillips. He told the AGM (1939) at the end of the Chamber's first year that there had been a danger of the town being bypassed but, due to communications between the Chamber and the Ministry of Transport, the proposed new road would not come into being for some years. Not everyone welcomed it with open arms in 1966, especially the shopkeepers and café and restaurant owners. Reg Thomas, secretary of the Honiton Chamber of Commerce, said 'We have to meet this challenge to our future prosperity – stand up and fight – or we sink.' One business that neither stood up and fought nor sunk was Quicksnacks in High Street, the first snack bar in the town. Realising that a bypass would mean their passing trade would indeed soon keep on passing, the owners converted it into the Whitewood Shop.

Traffic jams were by no means a modern curse in Honiton. Back in the pre-bypass days in 1930 there was concern over the volume of motor traffic through the town, which led to a census being taken at Easter. It was found to be exceptionally heavy and considerably in excess of that of previous years.

The check was taken for the week and the traffic through the town amounted to: Monday 14 April, 1,835 vehicles; Tuesday, 1,789; Wednesday, 2,197; Thursday 4,123 (the Easter build-up had begun); Good Friday, 5,010; Easter Saturday, 2,497. The previous year the figures had been 2,944 for the Thursday and 3,666 on Good Friday. The long-distance buses to Torquay and Plymouth were crowded but the weather was not all that welcoming, Honiton itself having blustery rain, and at nearby Luppitt there was two hours of snow.

Sadly there was a fatal accident, although it was not due to the increase in traffic through the town. Miss Selway, housekeeper to Mr F.W. Harding who lived in High Street, was fatally injured by a motor cycle just after ten o'clock on Thursday evening when attempting to cross the road opposite the Dolphin. Miss Selway, who was unconscious, was taken to Mr Helliar's shop where Dr Steele-Perkins saw her and ordered that she be taken to the infirmary. She died on the way.

Much earlier the Romans built their arrow-straight road to Exeter along what would one day become Honiton's High Street. The Romans left Britain in 410 – the Saxons began to arrive a century later to lay down most of the country's modern road system. Where two landowners' property met each would more than likely erect a hedge, the space in between being used as a path or lane. This is the reason why today, in many parts of Devon, you will suddenly come across a lane that starts and ends without a reason. They are parts of ancient Saxon 'lanes' that survived a later removal of one of the hedges along the rest of the 'lane' in the interests of increasing the size of a field. Several neighbouring fields were shaped to give each one access to a pond or a stream – a reason for the often bewildering twisting and turning of our hedges. Alternatively a hedge was planned to include a large boulder or tree stump rather than face the work necessary to remove it when woodlands were being cleared. All this in turn

This page: *Honiton's bridges over the River Otter in Edwardian times.*

The toll-'gate' at Holy Shute, c.1904. The area to the right has long since been built on.

Inhabitants of **HONITON** and its **Neighbourhood**, held the 13th day of **NOVEMBER, 1851**, at the **PUBLIC ROOM**, in Honiton, in pursuance of a Requisition to the Mayor of Honiton, most respectably signed, to take into consideration the subject of **RAILWAY COMMUNICATION** from **EXETER** through **HONITON**, to **YEOVIL**, and to adopt such Resolutions as may appear most adviseable for the purpose of the more speedily effecting a Railway through that important District.

The MAYOR in the Chair.

It was Moved by *Sir E. S. Prideaux, Bart.,* Seconded by *Captn. Basleigh,* and Resolved unanimously—That Railway accommodation will be of great service to this Town and Neighbourhood, and that the interests of the Town and Neighbourhood have hitherto been seriously affected by the want of it.

It was Moved by *Sir John Kennaway, Bart.,* Seconded by *Gustavus Smith, Esq.,* and Resolved unanimously—That having heard the statements made to this Meeting, we are of opinion that the Line from Exeter through Yeovil to Salisbury being the Central Line will be the most advantageous to this Town and the Public generally, as affording not only a shorter and therefore less expensive thorough Line from the West of England to London, to the Great Maritime Port of Southampton, to the South Coast of England and the Continent, but as opening up again the communication between the West of England, and the wealthy Trading Towns and fertile Agricultural Districts of Dorset, Somerset and Wiltshire from which we have of late been excluded.

It was Moved by *George Barons Northcote, Esq.,* Seconded by *The Rev. Thomas John Marker,* and Resolved unanimously—That a Deputation be appointed to wait (with the Deputations to be appointed at Yeovil or elsewhere) on the Directors of the South Western Railway Company, to urge upon them to co-operate with those Gentlemen who are now taking measures for applying to Parliament for the necessary Powers to form the Central Line of Railway, and that they will give them every support in their power.

It was Moved by *Charles Gordon, Jun., Esq.,* Seconded by *Col. Honywood,* and Resolved unanimously—That the best thanks of this Meeting be given to Mr. Locke, for attending the Meeting this day, and for the lucid and convincing statement he has laid before this Meeting, of the advantages which may be expected from the formation of the Central Line of Railway.

It was Moved by *Mr. Aberdein,* Seconded by *Captn. Basleigh,* and Resolved unanimously—That Sir John Kennaway, Bart., G. B. Northcote, Esq., Rev. T. J. Marker, Gustavus Smith, Esq., Col. Honywood, and Charles Gordon, Jun. Esq., with Joseph Locke, Esq., M.P., and Sir James Weir Hogg, Bart., M.P., be requested to act as the Deputation, to wait on the South Western Railway Company.

Edmd. STAMP, Mayor.

The Mayor having left the Chair, and J. W. Elliott, Esq., having been called thereto,

It was Moved by *Sir E. S. Prideaux, Bart.,* Seconded by *G. B. Northcote, Esq.,* and Resolved unanimously—That the best thanks of the Meeting be given to the Mayor, for his conduct in the Chair.

J. W. ELLIOTT, Chairman.

Below: *St Michael's Hill, now Church Hill, seen here c.1910; the left-hand side of the road has been developed.*

The Copper Castle toll-house and toll-gates, presumably after their closure in 1910, because no one is taking any payment from the occupant of the cart.

The Copper Castle viewed from an unusual angle on 26 March 1970.

The abolition of toll-gate charges in Honiton on 2 June 1910 led to considerable rejoicing and public entertainment.

helped give way to 'the rolling English drunkard and his rolling English road.'

Most of the English roads were dust bowls in summer and a sea of mud in the winter, and they remained as such until the eighteenth century when Turnpike Trusts were formed to raise the money needed for road improvements. The Honiton Turnpike was opened in 1754 which makes it (jointly with Axminster) the third oldest in Devon. The oldest was Stonehouse (opened in 1751, but closed in 1843) and then Exeter (1753). It might be of interest to learn that the Axminster Turnpike Trust covered more miles (141) than any other trust in Devon. Honiton's mileage was only 22. The term 'turnpike' stems from a person having to turn the spike in a spiked road barrier to gain passage, and the name stuck when gates were used.

During the nineteenth century some re-routing took place between Honiton and Axminster includ- ing, notably, a new road between Kilmington and Shute Pillars and another between Taunton Cross and Wilmington. Also, the new road was cut above Honiton between Mount Pleasant, strangely enough under the Axminster Turnpike Trust's authority, and the top of Axminster Hill in Honiton, where the Honiton Trust took over. The old road out of Honiton climbed up to where Manor House School is at the time of writing, following the line of the old Roman road as far as Mount Pleasant. It was proving to be too steep for the horses pulling the coaches and the new road was built below it with an easier gradient.

The Trust's income came from the rent of the gates,

which were offered at an annual auction when the rights to collect the tolls were sold to the highest bidder. Each gate was auctioned separately but there was nothing to stop one person winning more than one gate. Sometimes the rents that were paid quarterly were in arrears and had to be chased. The charges made by the Honiton Trust were similar to those for the Axminster Trust at Mount Pleasant and they were charged in a wonderful and bewildering way: for every horse or beast of draught drawing a coach, stagecoach, chariot, chaise, landau, etc, a charge of sixpence (2.5p) was made. But for a coach, chariot and chaise, etc, drawn behind or along with another such vehicle cost sixpence for four wheels and three pence extra for each additional two wheels. A loose mule or ass, laden or unladen and not drawing, only cost a penny. A horse or beast of draught drawing any wagon, wain, cart, etc with wheels of less than six inches in width cost sixpence. And it was also sixpence if four or less horses drew the cart with wheels of more than six inches in width. For some reason (probably a wider wheel caused less wear and tear on the road), if the cart had wheels of more than six inches in width and more than five horses it only cost five pence. Later, damage to the roads by locked wheels led to a regulation being introduced that skid-pans or slippers were to be placed at the foot of the wheel to prevent the road being damaged. A drove of oxen was charged at ten pence per score, and a drove of calves, swine, sheep or lambs only five pence a score. You could go back through the gate free of charge as long as you did so by nine o'clock

High Street on 16 November 1983. On the left is Dick Turner, a well-known Honiton character.

New Street in a quiet moment for traffic in 1982.

the following morning, and tolls were not collected on Saturdays or Fair Days. But try to avoid paying altogether and you could be fined as much as five pounds. Understandably, the king and his family went free, so did the Army, the local rector going to church or visiting the sick, and important people such as MPs. Free passage was also granted to hay, straw, wood, fruit and other produce not going to sale or market. The Royal Mail passed through toll-gates free of charge except at Mount Pleasant, where the Axminster Trust made a charge until 1811, when a bill was passed in parliament exempting the mail coaches from paying tolls at any of the Axminster toll-gates. This was done to bring it into line with the rest of the country.

Most of us have Christmas-card images of a coach careering over the snow with a trumpet blaring, but the trumpet (or horn) was only blown by Royal Mail coaches and only then to warn the gateman to have the gate opened so that the king's mail could pass through unhindered.

There were four mail coaches that passed through Honiton daily. Two of them were the Royal Mail coaches, one from London via Salisbury and Dorchester, the other from Exeter and the west; and there were two auxiliary mail coaches that came from Salisbury along the A30 to Crewkerne and then passed through Perry Street, Axminster and Honiton on its way to Exeter. There were also other private coaches that carried mail once a week.

When there was deep snow in Honiton the Honiton Trust paid the Board (Workhouse) for casual labour from the inmates. There were rules and regulations. No one could sell liquor from a toll-house. Neither could anyone break up or damage the road, and no person living beside any of the turnpike roads could have a gate that opened outwards. No one could allow blood [from a slaughterhouse] to run on to the road, nor kill, slaughter or singe on it, nor have bonfires or let off fireworks on it. In fact, no fires or

fireworks were allowed within 80 feet of the road. Digging pits for timber sawing was also not allowed.

To the uninitiated a timber pit was where two men sawed timber. The tree trunk, or whatever, was placed over the pit. One man held the saw above and pulled up, and the other man, in the pit, pulled the saw down. The bottom man's job was dusty and unpleasant, he was covered in sawdust, so the top man's job went to the senior of the two.

No football was allowed on the roads or, indeed any other game, and you could not leave a wagon or cart longer than was necessary for loading or unloading. No tents, huts, dung, manure, timber nor planks could be put along side the road. Again, you could be fined five pounds if you broke any of these regulations.

There were seven toll-gates or toll-bars around Honiton but only three survive in 2005, with the most striking being known as Copper Castle. This is an unusually crenellated building, hence its nickname, strategically placed just above the junction of Kings Road and Pine Park Road. At present (2005) it is painted in a rather striking shade of pink. Unusually, the tall windows serve both storeys. The building dates from at least 1809 when it was shown on the Ordnance Survey map. Subsequent road widening(s) means that the gates, if closed, would no longer reach one another.

There was some controversy in *Pulman's Weekly News* of 4 February 2004 over what was claimed to be a missing gate from the Holy Shute toll hut being found on a farm at Luppitt. The claim was described as 'almost frivolous' at a meeting of the Honiton Town Council's general purposes committee. Pictures dating from around 1900 show that there was not a gate at Holy Shute Cottage but a toll-bar with a hut to shelter the man who collected the tolls from people who entered the town by that route (from Monkton). It is wrongly called Holy Shute Toll Gate on a 1900 postcard. The hut at Holy Shute seems to be of a permanent nature. At the eastern end of the town there was

Above: *An aerial view of Honiton in 1966 just before the opening of the bypass, seen on the right. Much of the modern development in the top left-hand corner around Heathfield housing estate, the Blackberry industrial estate and the now Roman Way estate in the centre foreground around Read's garage (now two separate garage businesses – Renwicks Garage and Marsh Garage) are still green fields in this picture. Mawdsley's factory in the left foreground off Hale Lane (off picture) has been demolished and both it and the area to Hale Lane's left have also been developed. More or less dead centre the senior and junior schools can be seen and, some way behind them and to the left on the far side of Dowell Street, the open fields have been replaced by the Court House, a car park and the Oaklea housing estate.*

The civic launch for the new Honiton town bus in March 1989 by the mayor, Bob Walker. He is attended by the town crier, Joe Lake, with a crowd of VIPs waiting to be passengers for the first journey.

MINISTRY OF TRANSPORT

HIGHWAYS ACT, 1959

HONITON BY-PASS
HONITON BY-PASS, SIDE ROADS

THE MINISTER OF TRANSPORT hereby gives notice that he proposes to make the following Orders :—

1. An Order under s.7 of the above Act providing :—

   (a) that two roads which he proposes to construct at Honiton in the County of Devon shall become trunk roads on the date when the order comes into operation and

   (b) that the length of the London—Penzance Trunk Road to be superseded shall cease to be a trunk road on the 1st April next after the date on which notice is given by the Minister to the Devon County Council (who will become the highway authority responsible for that length) that the new roads are opened for through traffic.

2. An Order under s.9 of the above Act providing :—

   (a) for the re-alignment and regrading of eight lengths of highway which cross or enter the route of the above-mentioned by-pass;

   (b) for the construction by the Minister of seven new highways for purposes connected with the construction of the above-mentioned by-pass and in substitution for parts and lengths of existing highways authorised to be stopped up under the proposed Order;

   (c) authority for the stopping up of parts and lengths of highways which cross or enter the route of the above-mentioned by-pass;

   (d) that Devon County Council and the Honiton Borough Council shall become the highway authorities for the new highways within their respective areas on the date on which notice is given by the Minister to the Council concerned that the new highways are opened for through traffic.

COPIES of the draft Orders and of the relevant plans may be inspected free of charge at all reasonable hours from 8th May, 1962, to 8th August, 1962, at the offices of the Minister of Transport, St. Christopher House, (East Block G/14), Southwark Street, London, S.E.1., the Devon County Council, County Hall, Topsham Road, Exeter, Devon, the Honiton Borough Council, Municipal Offices, New Street, Honiton, Devon, the Divisional Surveyor, Devon County Council, Mill Street Depot, Honiton, Devon, and the Divisional Road Engineer, Government Buildings, Alphington Road, Exeter, Devon.

ANY PERSON may within three months from 8th May, 1962, object to the making of the Orders by notice to the Minister quoting reference HT 41/9/03 and stating the grounds of objection.

OLIVER COCHRAN,
1st May, 1962.   An Assistant Secretary

another such hut at the top of Bramble Hill that could be taken away. It was referred to, again on a postcard, as Bramble Hill Toll Gate but, like Holy Shute, there was only a toll-bar there. There were also gates, most probably bars, in Dowell Street, Clapper Lane and Northcote Lane. One of these three gates/bars must have been known as Potter's Kiln Gate, the name shown on the Honiton Paving Trust ticket.

The other two houses that survive along with Copper Castle are Stoneyford Bridge and Turks Head. The former is a two-storeyed building on the A373 towards Awliscombe that it is in a bad state of disrepair. The house at Turks Head is opposite the industrial estate built on the site of the old Heathfield Army Camp. All the gates became redundant on 31 May 1910 when the payment of tolls around the town was abolished. Two days later the entire town turned out for what proved to be long-remembered celebrations.

When the Honiton Town Council decided to sell all the gates and huts they kept Copper Castle to remain 'a memento of past times'. The local MP, Major Arthur Morrison Bell, who said he would donate £5 towards the proper upkeep of the gates, congratulated the council on this decision.

The Commissioners had needed to borrow over £6,000 pounds to get the gates up and running when the Trust was first formed. In March 1847, when the Turnpike Trust was transferred to the Town Council, that authority had to borrow £1,000 to keep things going. They had difficulty in meeting the loans and, in the end, agreed out of court to pay 10s. (50p) in the pound to the mortgagees.

Motor cars were not charged tolls when they began to appear on the roads around Honiton at the turn of the nineteenth century, although occasionally there were attempts to collect a toll from drivers. Another oddity was that a butcher, providing he was carrying meat in his cart, could come and go whenever he pleased, whereas a baker had to pay the tolls whether he was carrying goods or not.

The town clerk (Mr E.W. Hellier) was the man behind the abolition of the tolls. There was much praise for him in June 1847 when the gates were taken away. There were far less attractions (or should that be distractions?) in the early years of the twentieth century compared with today so much more was made of special days. Honiton declared a 'day of rejoicing' to mark the end of what was, at times, 'a source of annoyance to the inhabitants' of Honiton. All the shops closed at noon and a public luncheon and tea was held, and sports took place in the High Street. The mayor, Cyril Tweed, and Corporation had assembled at the Council Chamber and marched in procession behind the local Territorial Band. The mayor wore his handsome robes and gold chain, and was accompanied by Mr E.W. Hellier, the town clerk. On arrival at the Market House (later Woolworths and now a shopping arcade) the mayor stood on a wagon and read a fulsome proclamation to the gathered townsfolk. The mayoral party then went to the Dolphin Hotel for a public luncheon. The food had to be good; Alderman Banfield owned the Dolphin and any complaints would have been delivered with a right worshipful rebuke at the next council meeting. That evening about 700 children of the town were entertained at tea in the Market House.

The afternoon sports included a 100 yard, 200 yard, 880 yard and one mile race, and for the younger athlete there was a three-legged race and skipping race. There would have been a few bruises during the tug-of-war when teams were felled, even if the street was still unpaved. Fireworks were discharged at intervals and the band of F (Honiton) Company, Devon Regiment, under Bandmaster Ernest Arthur Connett, played for the dancing that followed until the National Anthem closed the festivities at 11p.m. You can rest assured that there were more than a few hangovers the following morning.

Mrs Frances B. Troup recorded (in the *Report and Transactions of the Devonshire Association*, 1898) that in the first half of the sixteenth century the road from Axminster did not come down Kings Road but followed the Shipley Lane as far as Copper Castle. The road then went across the present road and 'down Hale Lane to the old Taunton Road near Holy Shute.' She went on to say that:

... on entering the High Street, then nearly three-quarters of a mile in length, we would not have seen the broad highway of which the town is now so justly proud. It could have been no more than two lanes passing on each side of the low buildings that occupied the centre of the present street, with some intervening spaces from Allhallows Chapel to below the Dolphin Inn. The street too has been graded in recent times; the sharp decline to the foot of the Gissage must have been exceedingly steep. From an early time the little stream flowed through the town, perhaps not then confined on any conduit, nor furnished with dipping places, nor banked with green turf.

Nearly opposite the present market house stood the shambles, styled the 'tottering shambles' in 1807, but probably of comparatively recent erection at the period I am thinking about (1530). Behind them stretched a few houses, perhaps extending as far as Mr Murch's shop [?] even then. Lower down, on the north side, stood a flint-fronted house that belonged to the Abbot of Dunkeswell; this may be identified with the present post office building, which shows signs of having been erected in the sixteenth century [today, of course, the Post Office has crossed to the south side of High Street almost opposite St Paul's Church].

The worthy abbot may have already recognized the approaching wave that was to sweep him from his place, and sought, as many did at this period, to save

Above: *High Street on a market day, c.1900.*

Right: *High Street in 1910 on a market day.*

Below: *High Street, c.1900.*

Above: *West End, Honiton, in 1905. The Globe Inn was closed in 1972 and became a private residence; in 2004 it is the Society of Friends' Meeting Place. It had been called both the Carpenter's Arms and the Three Compasses in its earlier life.*

Left: *High Street in 1911; the three boys posing in the middle of the road would be in considerable danger there today.*

High Street (East End), Honiton in 1914.

New Street looking towards the town centre around 1912.

Looking into High Street from the west with the Rectory gate on the left. Both it, the trees and the Rectory itself were later demolished.

Right: *High Street, c.1920.*

High Street, c.1920 showing the cinema on the right with its feature board outside. It is hard to read what is on show but it does indicate that a lantern slide show of some description by the rector is on offer.

Above: *High Street, c.1920.*

Right: *High Street, looking west in 1926. Note what appears to be a delivery arm for a petrol pump on the left-hand side of the road.*

Below: *High Street just to the east of the New Street junction seen here in 1926. Of interest is that Dimond's, the printers and stationers, still trading in the same spot in 2005, operated a lending library at the time.*

Left: *High Street, Honiton, from the west, c.1925.*

Below: *Monkton Road around 1926.*

Left: *High Street in 1926.*

Moor's Garage, High Street, in 1926 with its petrol pump delivery hoses that could be swung out over the pavement to supply vehicles with fuel when needed. Post-war authority decided that they were a danger to the public and they were removed.

Above: *The High Street–Silver Street junction in the 1930s; no prizes for guessing whether the man pushing a small hand-cart on the right is selling ice-creams or sweeping the street.*

Left: *East End, Honiton, c.1930.*

High Street around 1930.

Honiton High Street in July 1963. Of special interest is the fact that the zebra crossing is without lights and has a much smaller central island and, happy days, there are two policemen controlling the traffic and the pedestrians. Also of interest is that traffic was still able to use Northcote Lane on the immediate right. On the left the sign of the now-closed Exeter Inn can be seen next to the overhead petrol pumps belonging to Read's Garage that used to be swung out over the pavement when pumping fuel into a car.

Looking up into High Street from West End in July 1973.

Above: *High Street seen on a market day in April 1977 when the stalls were on the pavement.*

Above: *The old pavements on the north side of High Street.*

Right: *Paul Carter of G. & H. Interiors inspecting the new kerbs in High Street in 1986.*

Below: *West End in April 1974, eight years after the bypass, and Honiton's main street is still a difficult place to navigate during the summer months. The tall brick building on the right, the Honiton Galleries at the time, was once the Devonia cinema.*

Above: *New Street seen in the 1970s when the white building in the left foreground was the council office.*

Left: *A snowy New Street seen here in 11 January 1982.*

Looking up New Street on a quiet day in February 1979.

That part of High Street between St Paul's Church and the entrance to Silver Street (just off picture on right) *in the 1980s.*

Honiton High Street on a market day in the 1980s. The stalls have encroached on the street. Also by this time Northcote Lane, to the left of Key Markets, must have been pedestrianized; otherwise the stalls would not have been allowed to block it.

Above: *Happily the old Pannier Market (on the left, pictured in 1991) has not been omitted from Honiton's pictorial history. Developed as a shopping precinct it bears the name of The Old Pannier Market Shopping Hall. Much of the New Dolphin Hotel has been developed, although the left-hand side of the former path to the stables at the rear (the archway) is still run as a hotel. That path to rear, and the rear itself, is now the Dolphin Court Shopping Precinct and Market.*

Left: *High Street in the early 1980s.*

Baxters' lorry is finding it difficult to make a delivery on a market day in December 1977.

Honiton Station, c.1905.

The Beech Walk between Honiton and Gittisham, a memorable sight in spring when the leaves have freshly opened.

something from the rapacious maw of Henry VIII. He placed property in the hands of some faithful layman. To the east of Tryppe's tenement stood the mansion house of the Courtenays, called 'Le Place' and evidently the greatest place in town. The gardens may have extended to the present Dolphin that takes its name from the badge of the Courtenay family.

On the south side of the street, nearly opposite, would have been the house soon afterwards occupied by the busy silversmith Murch, a Protestant refugee from Flanders, whose dependents still own the house [in 1898].

Near the market place would have been the stocks for the punishment of delinquents and at hand would have been the ducking pool – reserved for the punishment of women, and still in use in 1760 – and it may have had as a companion the scold's bridle. [Actually the ducking-stool would more likely have been further down the road by the Gissage – the nearest source of any water deep enough to duck a human being completely under the surface.]

Among the usual shops we would find those of the serge makers, but it was some years before another great manufacture of the town was introduced so we would look in vain for the place where James Rodge displayed his bone lace. The makers of this 'pretty toy' at a later date would have been found in the surrounding district, but doubtless when they brought their wares to town on market day they would take occasion to bathe their eyes, at the Holy Wells, at the east end of the town which by the faithful were believed to possess wonderful healing properties.

One of the considerable improvements to Honiton's main street came in 1823 when the Shambles were demolished. Another improvement finally arrived in 1920 when High Street was 'tar sprayed' – not before time. Before that, although roads were rolled flat, they were either muddy or dusty depending on the weather. In 1920 the Town Council discussed the particularly dusty conditions of High Street and the clouds of dust that constantly blew along it. The water-spraying cart had broken down and, faced with the cost of either repairing it or purchasing a new one, the Town Council decided to turn to tarmac.

The railways slowly killed off the coaching era but the more down-to-earth carrier and his cart that carried much of the countryside's commerce, and did so day in day out, week in week out, year in year out, summer and winter, sunshine and rain, survived. Their routes were often along roads that coaches never ever saw.

Thomas Hardy was talking of the unending cycle of England's agricultural year when he wrote 'Yet this will go onward the same tho' dynasties pass.' If the uncomprehending English labourers were capable of such thoughts, they would have said the same about the carrier. But they would have been just as wrong as Hardy had been about farming. The seeds of Britain's modern farming ways had already been sown. The farm labourer's year was bound in time-honoured traditions that dictated the time for ploughing, sewing, reaping, lambing, hay – the time for this and the time for that. People believed that would never change but slowly and surely machinery and improved stock, grass and corn strains and later, pesticides, altered the rest of England's farming ways forever.

In 1830 the railway age was already five years old, but the carrier's cart would resist it for almost another 100 years, and then it was the horseless carriage that finally killed it off. But it didn't disappear at first, the carrier still held sway and survived in East Devon until after the First World War. At this time thousands of redundant Army lorries became available at knock-down prices and the carriers at last plodded into history.

The railway arrived in Honiton in 1860 but it could have arrived some ten years earlier. The Great Western Railway fought against the so-called central route west of Salisbury, which would have been in direct opposition to their Paddington–Bristol–Exeter line (the northern route). The southern route was a non-starter from the beginning; no one ever came up with a definite suggestion, probably because the valleys that ran north from the English Channel defied any logical coastal line. At first it was denied that the district west of Salisbury was of sufficient

Honiton Station from the air in around 1930, showing the old covered footbridge. Much of the area to the right of the picture has been developed.

The old waiting-room at Honiton Station, 1970s.

Honiton Station in the 1960s. Note the gas lighting still in use.

Honiton Station from the up platform, 1960s.

The old Honiton Station is obviously in need of a facelift in this picture from the 1970s.

110

importance to warrant a railway, although it would have linked such towns as Yeovil, Chard, Axminster, Seaton, Sidmouth, Ottery St Mary, Budleigh Salterton, Broadclyst, Exmouth, Pinhoe and, of course, Honiton to both London and Exeter. An Act of Parliament of 1848 granted the South Western Railway the right to build the line, but by 1856 nothing had been done, mainly because the Great Western had fought tooth and nail against the proposal. A poster doing the rounds at the time claimed that:

Ten years have elapsed since the hostile policy of the Great Western Company succeeded in defeating the Bill before Parliament for a Central Line of Railway between London and Exeter.

During this interval every succeeding year has added a page to the history of a policy to which the West of England is indebted for being deprived of its just claims to be placed on the same footing with every other part of England, in respect of that most important part of local prosperity – Facility of Railway Communication.

To accomplish this object, every species of strategy which human ingenuity could conceive, all the professional talent which wealth could engage, all the personal and political influence which a powerful Company could exercise, have been brought to bear with the most indefatigable perseverance and unceasing assiduity.

In 1856 the Great Western even suggested that there be two railways running side-by-side and in competition to one another – one a broad gauge affair, the other narrow gauge. That idea was turned down and in 1860 the London and South Western Railway reached Honiton after accomplishing the considerable engineering feat of boring a mile-long tunnel under the 725-foot-high ridge of the Blackdown Hills around a mile to the east of Honiton Station.

One of the more unusual fires the Honiton brigade were called to, but unable to get a tender to the scene of, occurred in an old ventilation shaft for Honiton Tunnel in 1994. It turned the shaft into a 'giant kiln spewing clouds of toxic smoke', that took eight hours to bring under control. Originally the 220-foot-deep shaft was built to ventilate the tunnel on the Waterloo–Exeter line just over a mile to the east of Honiton Station. It was never completed because when the workmen met the greensand it kept falling in. A six-foot wall with a metal grille surrounded the top. When the Department of Transport announced their plans for the Honiton–Marsh dual carriageway and the A35 realignment to the east of the town, it was realised that the road might go over the shaft and it would have to be filled in. The first 60 feet was filled with gravel, and the next 140 feet with foam that solidified into a strengthening internal polyurethane sleeve. On the morning of the second day the workmen who returned to complete the last 20 feet discovered that dark-grey smoke was billowing through a hole that had been burnt in a temporary plastic cover. Because the fumes were toxic the police sealed off Northcote Hill and made house-to-house calls, warning residents that they should either leave or keep all doors and windows shut. Stock in nearby fields were moved and trains ran late, but firemen wearing breathing apparatus finally got the fire under control by using water-based expanding foam to shut off the oxygen supply. The cause of the fire was a complete mystery.

There is an old story that there was a skeleton at the foot of the old shaft. The legend persisted that there had been a gypsy camp at the top of Northcote Hill and when a gypsy was killed there in a fight his body was thrown down the shaft.

Edgar William Pulman reported in 1989 that:

The old building that housed the Booking Office, Waiting Rooms etc., and the Stationmasters' residence, no doubt built when the railway was opened, have been demolished and replaced by a ghastly modern building. Some years ago the double set of railway lines have gone [from Salisbury to Exeter Central] and there is now only one set of rails, except in the station.

Passengers alighting from the Up line have to cross by footbridge, as this is the only access to New Street. Years ago passengers alighting from the Up line had access into New Street through a gate at which there was always a ticket collector. After that the public went down a footpath beside the railway bank and through a gate into New Street. For some reason this was closed, now all the passengers have to use the footbridge.

In my days at Ottery King's School a large number of children went by train; a few cycled. We left Honiton at 7.40a.m. for Sidmouth Junction [now Feniton Station] where we had to wait about 45 minutes for a connection to Ottery St Mary. The same thing happened on the return journey; we left school at 4p.m. but did not arrive at Honiton until 5.30p.m.

The goods yard, now closed, was a very busy place. There were large stores for cattle feed, building materials and solid fuel. The railway lines enabled the goods trucks to be shunted the whole length of the yard and goods were unloaded into the stores. Miller & Lilley were the biggest concern and Mr Halse also had stores there. Blay's sawmills were also able to load timber into their wagons as their gantry was extended to reach the railway sidings. All these have now gone and goods are delivered by road. Most of the buildings have now gone but Bradfords have built a new showroom and offices.

Before and after. In the above picture, c.1958, the Black Lion Inn is closed and ready for demolition in the interests of road safety by widening the narrow entrance to New Street that is not wide enough to allow two vehicles to pass. In the later picture (below) the Black Lion has gone, part of giving New Street a second vehicle lane, the other part forming a small public area with seats, c.1964.

Chapter 13

Inns and Hotels

The claim was made in a 1951 report of a talk given by Mrs Wolsey Harris of Buckerell to the Rotary Club of Honiton (as taken from *Pulman's Weekly News*) that there were many inns in and around Honiton in 1530. It is certain that either different inns at different times bore the same name or many of the inns existed at later times than 1530. A total of 32 had been closed in the eighteenth century and in 1900 there were 25. In 1949 there were 15. The oldest recorded Honiton inn is the Angel (1605).

Signs had become compulsory for inns around 1330 and it is thought that the original Angel's sign originated from a religious picture of the Annunciation. Through weathering and exposure the central group vanished, leaving only the announcing messenger, the Angel.

Mrs Wolsey Harris claimed that the following inns existed in Honiton in 1530:

Anchor – on the south side of High Street, a nautical sign, the resort of sailors.
Angel Inn – recorded in 1605 but of earlier date, probably 1509.
Bell – an ecclesiastical sign and sometimes called the Six Bells.
Black Horse – north side of High Street, a very popular signboard.
Black Lion – closed in the interests of widening New Street in the twentieth century.
Blacksmith's Arms – a trade sign.
Blue Ball – in Northcote Lane.
Bull – resort of farmers on the north side of High Street, converted into a shop.
Clarence – named after the Duke of Clarence.
Chopping Knife – sometimes called the Chopping Knife and Rolling Pin. It was on the south side of High Street and, in 1951, was a lace shop.
Coach and Horses – on the south side of High Street.
Cock – on the north side of High Street and now (1951) a residence. The signboard depicted a cock saluting the dawn in the centre of the sun surrounded by sunrays.
Crown and Sceptre – on the south side of High Street between the Fountain and the Anchor.
Currier's Arms – alehouse in New Street, Mr Tweed's house in 1951. Another trade sign.
Dolphin – north side of High Street. A heraldic sign and the badge of the Courtenays, the lords of the manor. It was sold in 1922 for £5,700.
Dove – pulled down to make room for the building of

St Paul's Church.
Duke William's Head – now (1951) Mr Shute's office.
Exeter Inn – on the south side of High Street.
Fountain – south side of High Street and taking its name from its proximity to the town fountain.
George – north side of High Street. Now (1951) a shop, it was named as a compliment to the Hanoverian kings of Great Britain and also the patron saint of England.
Globe – north side of High Street and the sign of the Portuguese wine merchants.
Golden Lion – on the north side of High Street. The sign is that of the Royal Arms of England.
Green Dragon – either pulled down or destroyed by fire.
Greyhound – it was near the Shambles and burnt down.
Half Moon – in High Street and the Chapel Court and long since pulled down.
Half Moon – another Half Moon is said to have existed and was also pulled down.
Half Moon – an astronomical sign and pulled long-since down.
Hand and Pen – on the Exeter Road opposite the Whimple turning and some five miles from the town.
Hare and Hounds – north side of High Street and is now (1951) The Grove. It was burnt down.
Head and Horns.
Kings Arms – on the south side of High Street near the Chopping Knife. It is the second commonest sign and indicates loyalty.
King's Head – on the north side of High Street.
Lamb – on the south side of High Street; the sign indicated the Lamb and Flag, which was the sign of the Good Templars.
Malthouse – run by Goldsworthy in 1835.
Mermaid – in Northcote Lane, formerly called the Knacker's Hole it was next to the Knacker's Yard where the horses were slaughtered.
New Inn – usually among the oldest in a town and 'old with a new front'.
Old London Inn – at the east end of High Street and thus named because it was on the London Road.
Oxford – on the south side of High Street and with a possible connection to the Oxford Inn at Exeter.
Plough – the farmer's rest.
Pott House – in Clapper Lane and also called Sydenham's.
Railway – in Warwick Lane, in 1860 the London and South Western Railway reached Honiton on its way from Yeovil to Exeter.
Red Cow – on the north side of High Street, an alehouse at Radway.

A crowd outside the White Horse Inn that stood at the junction of High Street and Silver Street. The dress suggests late-Edwardian times, but the reason for the gathering can only be guessed at.

Left: *The White Hart Inn, High Street, c.1912. Of interest is the steamroller in the background, busily rolling the street.*

Right: *The Three Tuns Hotel in August 1954.*

Robert and Barbara Davidson, former owners of the Angel Inn, are seen here on 26 October 1990 presenting the Honiton coat of arms and a framed history of the town that had been in the bar of the hotel, to the Allhallows Museum. Receiving the coat of arms and history is John Yallop, museum curator. On the left is Mrs Betty Baker with Terry Glanvill behind the framed history.

This Hotel is owned and run by the family.

BARBARA and ROBERT DAVIDSON

BRENDA and RONALD KNIGHT

Angel Hotel
High Street
Honiton
Devon, EX14 8PE

Telephone
Management—Honiton 2829
Visitors—Honiton 2763
(STD 0404)

The Angel Hotel

HONITON, DEVON

LEE'S ANGEL HOTEL

HONITON.

Mrs. LEE,

Respectfully informs the Clergy, Gentry and Inhabitants of HONITON generally, that she has started an

OMNIBUS

To and from the STATION to meet every Train, and earnestly solicits their kind patronage.

THE OMNIBUS will be sent to any part of the Town for Passengers.---Fare Three-pence.

SUPERIOR

FLYS & CARRIAGES

to be had at the shortest Notice.

Angel Hotel, Honiton, July 19th, 1860.

KNIGHT'S GENERAL PRINTING-OFFICE, HONITON.

The Red Cow, High Street, c.1970.

High Street, c.1913, with the Dolphin Hotel on the left.

Red Hart and also the Royal Oak – sites unknown.

Red Lion – it had a striking signboard of 'good colour'.

Rose and Crown – an alehouse, site again unknown.

Star – in New Street.

Swan – north side of High Street; the heraldic badge of Edward III (1327–77) and of the Careys. Now (1951) known as Swan Yard and behind World's Stores.

Three Tuns – an old sign, taken from the arms of the Brewers' Company, incorporated 1579.

Turks Head – on Exeter Road and sometimes called Saracen's Head. It became a road house. Tokens are known to exist.

Union House – site unknown but certainly not for the inmates of the Workhouse.

Vine – north side of High Street and the emblem of the liquor trade or an inn in a garden or vineyard (an old name for an allotment).

Vintner's Arms – a wine house owned by Mr Walter Harris and converted into a dwelling.

Volunteer – in High Street.

White Hart – north side of High Street and now (1951) next to Mr Yates's corn shop.

White Horse – at the eastern end of Silver Street.

White Lion – south side of High Street, badge of Edward IV (1660–83, exiled 1670–71).

Wine Cellar and Vaults – opposite the Shambles and owned by John Duke.

The inns of which references were found after the above list was published were:

Acland Arms – this held a licence in 1870.

Apothecaries Arms – William Derby issued a ^{1}/$_2$d. token for this inn (1663).

Drewe – later the Midland Bank.

Golden Fleece – a token was issued for this place but no details survive.

Hall's Inn – John Hall issued a ^{1}/$_2$d. token in 1663.

Hare and Hounds – an unrecorded inn on the site of the late Dr Hoffman's residence, The Grove.

Hat and Feathers – the sign represented a low-crowned hat with a feather; John Hall issued a ^{1}/$_2$d. token in 1664.

Lion Inn – a lion passant guardant; Samuel Powning issued a ^{1}/$_2$d. token in 1663.

Oxford Inn – an old inn that occupied the site of the present (2005) White Lion. 'Its license was forfeited as a disorderly house.'

Phoenix – a mythological sign usually used by Chemists, Richman's and now [1951] the International Stores.

Pressing Iron and Shears – no details.

Sachell's Inn – Roger Sachell issued a token in 1667; sign unknown.

Salters' Arms – Thomas Ash issued a token in 1664. Honiton was on the route taken by the salt trade from Budleigh's (later East Budleigh) salt pans and it is

Above and right: *The Turks Head road house, Exeter Road, c.1934.*

Below: *Some of the attractions at the Devonia cinema in Honiton in April 1936.*

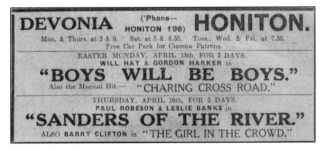

possible it was an overnight stop for the carriers.

The Bottle – unusually so, this inn has had three name changes: Anchor, Bottle and White Lion. A deed stated that is was 'formerly the White Lion Inn but for many years a private residence', and now (1951) Woodstock.

Three Cups – on the north side of High Street, it was mentioned in a deed dated 1790 and it occupied the site of what became the Devonia cinema. In 1736 it was owned by Thomas Vickers and later became a butcher's shop (Mr Hartnell's).

Vintners' Arms – Walter Harris was the licencee and now (1951) it is the Central Meat Shop.

The Dolphin Inn, now sadly closed, has a history befitting one of Honiton's oldest inns and changed its name to the Dolphin Hotel sometime after 1770. It was following the example of the Dolphin in Exeter, said to be the first in England to assume the title of hotel. If this is correct Honiton's Dolphin Hotel is among the very earliest to do so as well.

The tokens that some of the inns are known to have issued were in lieu of coins of the realm which were not always available. They were given as change and were redeemable throughout Honiton.

This practice was common throughout England.

Baring-Gould, writing around the turn of the nineteenth century, recorded:

The Dolphin, Honiton's principal inn is supposed to still possess some portion of the ancient building belonging to the Courtenays, whose cognisance is the inn sign, the Dolphin. On one of the walls there is a shield of arms borne by the Courtenays of Powderham in the fourteenth century.

From the following quotation it can be seen that Philip Courtenay had a residence in the town of Honiton:

In 1402 Leonard, the Abbott of Newenham, was forcibly abducted together with two of his monks, from the abbey by Sir Philip Courtenay and an armed force of sixty men. They were brought to Honiton and confined in Sir Philip's house for fifteen days. For this, and other offences Sir Philip was imprisoned in the Tower of London during the King's pleasure.

In 1688 Colonel Tollemache and his staff occupied the Dolphin. It was the time of the Glorious Revolution and William of Orange's landing in Torbay on

5 November. James II stated in his memoirs that the events that happened in Honiton and the news from the Dolphin were 'the turning point of his fortunes'.

Many other notable people have stayed at the hotel, including Lord Cornbury (later the Marquis of Malmesbury) who wrote 'Lilliburlero', the ballad that was sung by the entire army in 1688. Others were Lord Colchester (later Lord Rivers); Colonel Godfrey, who married Lady Arabella Churchill (by whom the Duke of York – later James II – had previously had four children); the sister of the Duke of Marlborough who was born some ten miles away at Ash House in Musbury. Sir William Yonge, the great minister, and George III (1760–1820) and Queen Charlotte, along with three of their daughters, received the loyal greetings of the people of Honiton outside the inn on their way to stay with Sir George Yonge, Secretary of State for War, at Escot House in 1798. In 1833 George III's granddaughter, the then Princess Victoria, took refreshment inside while the horses were being changed.

The Knacker's Hole was said to be Honiton's oldest inn after the Dolphin and its far from salubrious surroundings were matched by the signboard, which depicted a gruesome dead horse. James Smyth was landlord there in 1660 and, in his unfinished will he left 20 shillings (£1) to be distributed to the poor of the town after his death in 1677. It seems that the will, being unsigned, was written on his deathbed and the poor of Honiton probably never got the 20 shillings. The gruesome name and signboard may not have worried Smyth but his daughter Ann became landlady in 1700 and the name (and signboard) was changed to Mermaid.

The Dolphin did not get all the big 'names'. Charles Dickens visited the Golden Lion in 1835 when he was a reporter for a London newspaper. He called there on his way back to London after covering the General Election at Exeter (Mrs Wolsey Harris claims that it was the Exeter Assizes but there was a General Election in 1835), but promptly left when he saw a rival London reporter entering behind him. He wanted the scoop and after changing horses he hurried off – without his dinner!

There was a pecking order for the inns on market days when 'My Lady went to the Angel, My Lord to the Rose and Crown and the farm boy to the Rolling Pin and Chopping Knife.' He knew his place and never ventured near the Dolphin. In any case he got tasty pasties at the Rolling Pin and Chopping Knife; the signboard told him so – between the two symbols was a big pasty.

The police asked the Honiton Brewster's Sessions to close the Black Lion Inn on Wednesday, 5 March 1913. But they were turned down, the happy little pub living on until around 1960 when it finally went in the interests of road safety when the entrance to New Street was widened.

Back in 1913, when Honiton's population was 3,191, there were 22 fully licensed houses in the town, two with six-day licenses and two beerhouses. There was one licensed house for every 145 members of the town's population, and that is not counting the six-day licensees nor the beerhouses (lucky Honitonians!).

Superintendent Coles told the magistrates that the Black Lion was situated at the junction of High Street and New Street (something they knew as well as he did) and that it was a fully licensed house owned by John George Hann of the Honiton Brewery, with Arthur Hartnell as the licensee. He also carried on in business as a butcher. The Black Lion was a tied house with a rateable value of £36 and a rental of £45. There were 12 large rooms, seven of them available for the public. There was stabling for 17 horses at the rear and also five loose boxes, together with a large shed and slaughterhouse and a large yard to which four other people had a right of way. The interior of the house was in a bad state of repair and much renovation was needed. The sanitary conditions, usually a favourite ground for police objections, were said to be good. The pub had four entrances, two from New Street, one from High Street and one from King Street.

The police agreed that Mr Hartnell was a good landlord but pointed out that the Exeter Inn was only 14 yards away, the Dolphin 16 yards, the Vintners' Arms 24 yards and the Angel 26 yards. In all there were 11 licensed houses within 120 yards. Superintendent Coles said that personally he thought that the Black Lion was necessary (so why was he objecting?) and the magistrates renewed its licence, as well as that of the Exeter Inn.

Also up before the magistrates that day were the Anchor, the White Hart, the Vintners' Arms and the Exeter Inn. When the police objected to the Vintners' Arms' license being renewed they went through the same 'so many yards from' rigmarole all over again. Mine host at the Vintners' was Walter Willey who had his case referred to the Devon Licensing Committee at Exeter in June, along with that of the Anchor and the White Hart. All three lost their day in court but the respective landlords or landladies, Walter Willey (Vintners' Arms), Mrs Holway (Anchor) and Mrs Kitty Cheeseworth (White Hart), were compensated for their loss of income.

No one thought of mentioning it at the time, but Honiton's population was still 3,191 and there were still 19 fully licensed houses in the town, two six-day licenses and two beerhouses, which meant that every 167 Honitonians still had a pub to themselves – or every 138 Honitonians if you throw in the six-day pubs and the two beerhouses.

In 2005 Honiton has ten pubs or hotels: Carlton, Dolphin, Honiton Motel, Railway, Red Cow, Star, Three Tuns, Vine, Volunteer and White Lion. If you add the various clubs to them (the Working Men's

Club, the Conservative Club, Honiton Royal British Legion Club and the clubhouses of the golf, rugby, bowling clubs) and Mountbatten Park, that houses the football and cricket clubs (one has to be a paid-up member to visit any of the clubs) there is now only one pub for every 555 Honitonians.

Speaking at a meeting of Honiton Rotary Club in 1960, Mrs A. Wolsey Harris of Splatt Hayes, Buckerell, said:

Honiton's geographical position made it one of the centres of western travelling, it being near Exeter, which was the key to the west, as the centre of the woollen trade which was so prosperous in the fifteenth and early sixteenth centuries. The inn was the lodging place for travellers; the tavern a drinking place where business was transacted; a bush house was a place where beer or cider was sold without a licence on festive occasions, such as a fair, when a bush was hung out of a window.

She quoted an old writer (Andrew Borde) who wrote in the eighteenth century that:

Ale was made of malte and water; and they the which do put any other thing to the ale except yest barme or godegood does spoil their ale. Ale for an Englyshe man is a natural drink; it must be fresh and clear, not ropy or smoky, and shout be dronke under v days olde, new ale is unwholsome and sowre ale and dead ale is no good for a man. In the monastries the allowance per day per head was a gallon, with a second gallon of weak ale called 'shipman' ale.

In the reign of Edward I (1277–1307), Isabella de Fortibus, as Lady of the Town of Honiton, claimed to have return of the writs, gallows, assize of bread and beer, a pillory, a ducking stool and free warren which priveliges the Jury presented to her. Fresh brews of ale had to be tested by the ale-conner or taster, who was

summoned by the simple method of hanging a bush at the end of a long pole called an ale-stake. It is told that a certain Honiton brewer, who sold bad beer, was punished by being compelled to drink a draught of his own brewing, and having the rest pored over his head; and while they were about it they punished the alewives as well.

This was when the beveridge approached too much in quality of the light dinner-ale of today. They ducked the alewive, which was much worse than drinking a draught, for they knew her capabilities only too well. A gallon of ale, more or less, was no punishment for her, so they put her in the ducking stool and gave her a dip in the River Gieage [sic] at the foot of the hill in Honiton.

The ducking-stool was 'a fearsome machine' that the writer Berreti described in his *Journey from London to Genoa* in 1770.

At Honiton we went as far as a small rivulet, the Gissage, where I took notice of an engine called a Ducking Stool. A stool to sit on, a kind of armed chair of wood fixed at the extremity of a pole fifteen feet long. The pole is horizontally fixed on a pole just by the water and loosely pegged to that post, so that by raising it at one end you lower the other end down into the widest part of the rivulet. The stool was later used for ducking scolds. At that time there was no bridge over the Gissage.

It is said that the 'old witches were ducked several times.' The last person to be ducked was a woman who was found drunk on a Sunday morning in the cellar of a Mr Gibbons in 1770. The stocks stood close to Allhallows and their last occupant was a vagabond called Charles Ford in around 1812. In 1823 the stocks, the ducking-stool and the pillory were all taken away.

The Carlton Café towards the eastern end of High Street seen here in the 1930s. It became a pub towards the end of the 1970s.

The Manor House Hotel, High Street, in 1984 when it had been converted into offices.

Above: *Foale's Grocery & Provision Stores, c.1923.*

Left: *The Honiton Lace Shop, High Street in August 1992.*

Below: *The Honiton Lace Shop, High Street, c.1950.*

Chapter 14

Industries

Honiton Lace

Honiton lace was once made in almost every town, village and hamlet in East Devon. Cosimo de Medici, writing of his travels around England in 1669, said that there was not a cottage in Devon where white lace was not made in great quantities. This may not be strictly true, but at one time Honiton was said to have 1,341 lace workers, Ottery St Mary 814, Seaton and Beer (one parish at the time, although Seaton was to grant Beer its independence later) 326, and Sidmouth 302. The economies of the smaller villages also depended to a great extent on the trade and there were 114 workers at Upottery, 72 at Axmouth and 70 at Farway.

It is claimed, surely apocryphally, that it was known as Honiton lace because it was dispatched from that town to London by coach and on arrival the merchants would ask for 'the boxes from Honiton'. That is a good story, and often told, but the late John Yallop, an eminent researcher into the story of Honiton lace and formerly the curator of the Allhallows Museum in the town, once told me that there was not a shred of truth in the claim.

What is true is that the fine quality of the lace attracted royalty – and there was none more royal than Queen Victoria who included Honiton lace made in Beer as part of her wedding dress when she married Albert. It cost her £1,000 and, according to the *Morning Post*:

The lace intended for Her Majesty's bridal dress though properly called Honiton Lace, was worked at the village of Beer, which situated near [sic] the sea is about ten miles from Honiton. It was executed under the command of Miss Bidney, a native of that village, who went to London at the command of Her Majesty.

More than a hundred persons were employed upon it from March to November last year. These poor women derive a scant existence from making lace, but the trade has so lately declined that had it not been for the kind consideration of Her Majesty in ordering this dress they would have been destitute this winter.

No one can form an idea of the gratitude they expressed, who has not heard of it from their own lips. The lace, which is to form the flounce of the dress, measures four yards and is three-quarters of a yard in depth. The pattern is a rich and exquisitely tasteful design, drawn expressly for that purpose and surpasses anything that has been executed in either England or

Wales. So anxious has the manufacturer been that Her Majesty should have a dress perfectly unique, that she has, since the completion of the work, destroyed all the designs. The veil, which is of the same material and made to correspond, has offered employment to the poor lace workers for more than six weeks. It is a yard and a half square.

If the dress cost £1,000, and if there were more than 100 people employed on it, after the cost of the materials are taken into account the workers would have picked up around a pound each. This hardly went to make a Happy Christmas for them, although the Queen did send £10 down to Beer to pay for a tea party for the women who had worked on her lace. Jane Bidney herself went to London to meet Queen Victoria and while she was waiting to be presented she fainted; later she attended the wedding.

There has been a considerable royal connection with Honiton lace. Before Victoria's wedding Queen Charlotte, wife of George III, had commissioned a dress and Queen Adelaide, Victoria's aunt and the wife of William IV, ordered her wedding lace from Mrs Lathy of Honiton. Queen Adelaide's order had been as a response to a petition from the workers; it incorporated flowers, the initial letter of each spelling out the name Adelaide: Amaranth, Daphne, Eglantine, Lilac, Auricula, Iris, Dahlia and Eglantine again.

Queen Victoria continued to support the industry and bought the christening shawl for her first son, later Edward VII, from the town. It has been used at every royal christening since then. She also ordered a handkerchief and a black shawl, most likely after the death of the Prince Consort. The weddings of the Princess Royal, Princess Alice and the Princess of Wales (later Queen Alexandra) also brought trade to the town.

Queen Elizabeth, the Queen Mother, received a handkerchief from Mrs Allen of Beer in 1939; Princess Margaret was given a lace bonnet and Queen Elizabeth II received a tray with a Honiton lace centrepiece to mark her 21st birthday in 1947. The speaker of the House of Commons, Bernard Weatherill was presented with a lace jabot (an ornamental frill for the front of his shirt) on a visit to Honiton and, later, some lace cuffs. When Queen Elizabeth, the Queen Mother, and her husband, George VI, made a state visit to Canada and the USA, she was given some lace from Beer to give as a present to Mrs Roosevelt.

A Beer lacemaker, who helped to make Queen Victoria's wedding dress.

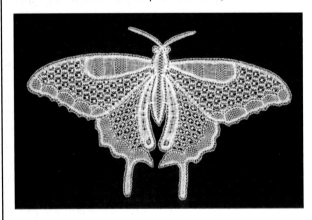

Above and right: *Honiton Lace designed and made by Pat Perryman and on view at the Allhallows Museum, Honiton.*

Left: *Mrs Fowler was one of Honiton's best-known lacemakers in early-nineteenth-century Honiton and held royal warrants from both Queen Mary and Queen Alexander. She had also held one from Queen Victoria and was patronised by HRH Princess Louise.*

One of the best known and most respected of Honiton lace manufacturers in Edwardian Honiton was Mrs Ann Fowler, of whom the *Whitehall Review* said in 1912:

To the lay mind, the quality of lace revolves itself dimly into machine-made versus hand-made, but to the expert, the art lover, the priestess of the innermost of mysteries, such a division savours of profanation. To such there can be no question of the comparatively harsh texture of pedantic regularity of the machine-made commodity. To connoisseurs the term lace can only apply to the fairy flowers and the cobweb rescan, the direct outcome of skilful human fingers plying bobbin or needle.

'Distinquez, distinguons,' as old French philosophers say. Among the hand-made beauties of lace, let us differentiate them into beautiful, more beautiful, most beautiful. In the superlative category lies the exquisite handiwork of Mrs Fowler and her two nieces, Misses B.D. and G.L. Ward. Frankly, those among us who have not been privileged to have seen the work of these skilled craftswomen, and are only acquainted – to its prejudice – with the Honiton of ordinary commerce cannot have any conception of the possibilities of the lace, the originalities and beauty of design, the delicacy of the marvellous stitches, the airy elegance of the finished weft.

Indeed, between the heavy, often grotesquely, clumsy, uninspired Honiton patterns as exhibited in drapers' shops, and the valuable and beautiful Garniture produced by these past-mistresses of the art of lace-making, there is decidedly less resemblance than that existing between a broken-down cab-horse and a high-mettled thoroughbred racer. This characteristic and national lace has gone through many and varied vicissitudes in its time, but, greatly owing to the Royal patronage, and to the inde-fatigable efforts of those ladies in originating new styles and stitches, [it] has, during the Victorian era, regained general esteem, and is at this moment at the height of its popularity. It is interesting to remember that her late Majesty Queen Victoria's wedding dress was composed entirely of Honiton sprigs and cost one thousand pounds. The sprigs were connected by a variety of openwork stitches, but the pattern was destroyed immediately the dress was completed.

The wedding dresses of Queen Alexandra and the Empress Frederick and the Princess Alice were all made or trimmed with Honiton lace. Her Majesty Queen Alexandra's had Prince of Wales feathers mixed with ferns, which had an excellent effect. In 1850 Queen Victoria confirmed the Royal warrant given to Amy Davey, née Lathy, by Queen Adelaide. Mrs Ann Fowler has been repeatedly favoured with Royal Warrants. Her late Majesty, Queen Victoria, conferred this distinction upon her in 1882.

In 1901, Mrs Fowler again received this honour from Her Majesty Queen Alexandra, and in 1904 Queen Mary [then Princess of Wales] also made Mrs Fowler her lace-maker by Royal warrant.

The popularity of this beautiful lace has been greatly revived of late years by this royal patronage, and locally by the assistance of Lady Peek and Mrs Bernard. The Devon County Council has also done good work in promoting the development of the industry, by which the quality of the thread and the design has been greatly advanced.

This Mrs Fowler was one of two sisters who had their lace shop next to the Manor House in High Street, which was for many years the home of the Honiton Rural District Council. In around 1920 they moved to a new shop at the eastern end of High Street and on the opposite side of the road where, unlike the shop next to the Manor House, it had 'back sun' and the delicate lace was less likely to get too much exposure to the sunlight.

One could say that the Duke of Alba was the father of the Honiton lace industry because it was his persecutions that caused the Flemish refugees to flee to England where many settled in the West Country. Many local names stem from these Flemish origins such as Trump, Murch and Gerrard. Claims have been made that my own Gosling name owes its origins to the Huguenots, but because my ancestors are recorded in the Colyton parish register as early as 1540 in various forms, Goslin, Gosland, Joslin, Goscelyn and Gosling, I doubt that it is true.

Of course lace was made in England before the arrival of the Flemish workers, but it was needle lace as opposed to the newcomers' pillow lace that used bobbins and very fine thread. The refugees brought the art of lacemaking with them; Honiton work being very much like Flemish lace. Because Honiton was the centre of the trade in East Devon it became known as Honiton lace but was known locally as bone lace as well, because the workers used bobbins made out of bone and pinned the lace to the cushion with fish-bone needles.

The 'secrets' of the trade were passed down from parent to child and lace schools were introduced where, at first, the children worked from ten until noon; later they would face the full eight-to-eight day. They started at around five years old, being apprenticed to a teacher for two years. The teacher kept the lace they made and also received a small fee. Once the apprenticeship was over the lace became the property of the child but he or she paid around 4d. a week depending on how much teaching he was still receiving.

The industry was of such importance to East Devon that a petition protesting against the repeal of the 1697 Act, that granted English lace protection against foreign imports, was sent to parliament.

Like so many trades the introduction of a cheaper, although not necessarily better, substitute led to the decline of the Honiton lace trade. The biggest blow came in 1818 when, after being driven out of Loughborough by Luddites who destroyed his factory,

John Heathcoat opened a new factory at Tiverton. He was able to produce machine-made net at a much lower cost than the local handmade product.

Not unnaturally the East Devon lacemakers cut corners in order to try to compete with Heathcoat's product. They used as few pins and bobbins as they could, worked with the coarsest of thread and the simplest of patterns. So poor did their work become that the Honiton workers themselves called their own product 'rag lace'.

As an industry lacemaking no longer exists in and around Honiton, but interest in the local lace remains high, so much so that demonstrations of the art are held regularly at the Allhallows Museum where there are also classes in lacemaking. The museum has an outstanding collection of lace pieces and it is well worth the modest entrance fee to go and see it. Among the pieces there is one that took 3,000 hours to make and a wedding veil that cost £84 in 1869. Perhaps the most interesting is the 6-foot long flounce that was designed especially for Queen Victoria's youngest son Leopold, who was born in 1853. It was made by a Mrs Twyford of Exeter, Honiton lacemaker by appointment to Queen Victoria. Prince Leopold suffered from the blood disorder haemophilia and died after an accident in 1882, two years after his marriage to Princess Helena of Waldeck-Pyrmont. Princess Helena bequeathed the flounce to her grandson Leopold, Duke of Saxe-Coburg-Gotha, who sold it in London after the Second World War. A private collector, Margaret Simeon, bought it and when her collection was sold at Phillips in London in 1992 it was acquired by the museum for £4,000. As well as the museum a visit should be made to the Honiton Lace Shop at 44 High Street. Much of its business is done via the internet (www.honitonlace.com) but the proprietor, Jonathan Page, welcomes callers by appointment.

Honiton Pottery

Although, sadly, Honiton pottery is no longer made in the town, its origins can be traced back at least as far as 1643 when a mention of the trade is made in the churchwarden's accounts. In 1881 James Webber built the pottery at the eastern end of High Street after operating from another pottery in the town. In 1918 Charles Henry Fletcher Collard, a potter of considerable experience (having been in business as a potter at Aller Vale, Torquay, and then Poole, where he founded his Crown Dorset Art Pottery in 1905) acquired the business. He found himself in a primitive world at the Honiton pottery where there were no toilets (water had to be carried from a nearby stream for use in the pottery) and the gas lighting was hardly bright enough for the workers. He modernised the place, but carried on using the clay from a 30-foot seam at the back of the buildings. He also used different

The Honiton Pottery Shop in 1991, a time when it was possible that it was going to be turned into a housing estate.

coloured clays from other parts of Honiton, including attractive white clay from Dowell Street.

This is not the place to give a lengthy description of the methods of firing the kilns, of producing the finished product, or of the many people who worked for Collard, all of whom always spoke of him as a very good employer. If you are interested in the subject you can do no better than read Carol and Chris Cashmore's *Collard, the Honiton and Dorset Potter*. Published in 1983 it might be difficult to find a copy in the bookshops, but the Devon County Library has one.

Keith Luxton bought the business in 1947 and continued production until 1991. Then, because of a failure to find a site for relocation in Honiton, which was needed in an expanding postwar market, production was transferred to the Dartmouth pottery, which retained the title of Honiton pottery and sold it via the High Street shop. Sadly again, although that shop still sells pottery, Honiton pottery is no longer available.

Blay's Sawmills

The sawmills were opened in the middle of the nineteenth century and were first owned by the Buckingham family. When the last of the Buckingham's retired in 1917 the machinery was steam driven and transport and haulage was provided by the firm's own stables, which housed 26 horses. George Blay bought the mill in 1917; he employed several managers but had trouble in finding a suitable one until John Maeer was engaged. He had previously been with Heal's Sawmills at Axminster and was given a year to reorganise the mill and show a profit, which he certainly did, although Mr Blay died soon after he arrived. Other directors, including Mrs Blay, took over and eventually Jack Maeer followed his father as manager and became managing director when Blay's became a limited company. The mills were closed in the 1990s and the site was developed.

During the Second World War the mill was burnt

Above: *Decorators are seen here at work at Honiton Pottery in the 1930s. Left to right, back row: Joan Collard (standing), Beryl Radford, Edith Redhead, Linda Marks, Dorothy Channon, Vera Stuart; front row: Peggy Cooper, Florrie Loving, Jessie Bambury.*

Right: *Paul Redvers (right), managing director of Honiton Pottery, and company designer Martin Lloyd with the design being used on the company's royal wedding pottery in April 1986.*

The presentation to the mayor, Reg Thomas on 30 March 1970 of a Honiton Pottery commemorative plate marking the 350th anniversary of the departure of the Pilgrim Fathers. Also in the picture are the owners of the Honiton Pottery, Mr and Mrs Paul Redvers.

George Blay Ltd, Marlpits Lane, seen from the air around 1952.

to the ground on a Saturday night, the cause of the conflagration being an electrical fault igniting sawdust under the floor. The building was then constructed of timber and in a short time was blazing from end to end.

It was during that period that the Luftwaffe was bombing Cardiff and it was feared that if a raid was made that night the German bombers might drop their bombs on Honiton instead. It was said at the time that in order to prevent this happening fighter aircraft circled the town throughout the night.

The very next day a large shed was cleared and within a few days saw benches were installed and men were working there. Planning permission to rebuild was sought and obtained and, although building materials were in short supply, the fact that the sawmill would provide much-needed timber for the war effort eased the way. The mill was completely rebuilt and new machinery installed. The business was closed in the late 1990s and the site was developed.

Honiton's Milk Trade

Collecting milk bottles might not register very high on the list of Britain's most favourite hobbies but Honitonian Peter Hayward, who has spent many years in the milk trade, has devoted much of his time to their study and to the evolution of milk delivery to the doorsteps of East Devon. I am grateful to be allowed to use his notes.

During the 1940s and early 1950s there were probably 15 dairies in and around Honiton, some of them, of course, going back to pre-war times. Peter mentioned Cotfield Dairy at Cotfield Farm in Langford Road, and Jim Rosewell's Dairy at 60 High Street, which Cecil Harris had taken over from the Maynards. And there was Charlie Connett, who operated in King Street, Cranford Dairy, High Street, which belonged to Mr G.K. Williams and Cowley Dairy, in Silver Street that was owned by Mr J. Durbin.

Out at Combe Raleigh Mr Lodwig ran a dairy and, before we come back into town, there was the Rounsevell family who delivered milk out of Elmfield Farm Dairy at Weston. Just back from the road, and now flanked by Honiton's bypass, we found Roebuck Farm from where John Underdown started delivering milk in 1952 when he bought a 27-gallon daily milk round from J.K. Williams of Cranford Dairy. This milk was raw and unpasteurised and sold in half-pint, pint, 1.5-pint and 2-pint bottles. He then purchased Charlie Connett's gallonage in 1954.

Back in town Mrs Madge operated the dairy shop at 191 High Street (Wickham Antiques in 2005); Mrs Proll ran the Anchor Dairy on the opposite side of High Street at No. 178 while, further down Honiton's main street could be found the Westlake Dairy (No. 118) and the London Dairy (No. 49).

At 19 New Street Mr Griffin owned the New Street Dairy; in Central Place, Wallace Cole ran the Central Dairy and, out at Kings Arms Farm in Exeter Road, was another dairy which belonged to Mr R.W. Cole.

By 1952 these 15 dairies had dwindled to just five: Roebuck Dairy, the Honiton Dairy at 60 High Street, New Street Dairy, Central Dairy, where Wallace Cole had given way to George Carter, and Mr Lodwig at Combe Raleigh. Even with only five dairies now delivering milk in Honiton, it was still quite common to see as many as five different milkmen delivering down most streets in Honiton, quite often at the same time.

This problem continued until 29 November 1966 when the East Devon Dairies (EDD) was formed by the amalgamation of the Roebuck Farm, Honiton, New Street and Central Dairies. Mr Lodwig sold his Combe Raleigh business to the Co-operative Society in 1967.

The EDD bought its pasteurised milk from Hammett's Dairy in Exeter who delivered it to a communal fridge in Dowell Street car park until 1980. EDD went from strength to strength, buying out Briggs Dairy at 11 Jesu Street in Ottery St Mary in 1961, where Cecil Harris was engaged as manager. This enabled them to get a foot in the Sidmouth area. John Underdown's three children all helped with the milk deliveries while his wife was involved with the dairy side of the business for several years. Raw, unpasteurised milk would continue to be sold and bottled by EDD until 1993, although sales gradually diminished in favour of pasteurised milk.

A major change in the business occurred in 1980 when John Underdown bought out the retail liquid milk interest of all the remaining dairies and set up a new depot in King Street, next to Hillside Garage with a three-year lease from G.H. Baker, the local butcher and abattoir operator. The United Dairies (Wholesale) Ltd butter factory closed but Express Dairy opened their new premises in Ottery Moor Lane in 1969, where the majority of the locally produced milk was processed. Sadly, Express Dairy closed the plant in 1992 as part of a rationalisation programme linked to the national decline in butter sales and the Intervention Board plans.

The EDD depot in King Street operated for around three years. During this time the Underdown family planned a new processing plant at the Heath Park industrial estate to pasteurise and bottle milk and become a local independent processor. The venture was scheduled to start up in 1984 with the introduction into the West Country of low-fat milk.

This necessitated additional equipment and EDD was one of the first processors in the West Country to have its own separator and homogeniser, which provided a surplus of cream for sale to other outlets such as hotels, shops, Exeter University and the East Devon Health Authority.

The new dairy came on line in 1984, at a time when EDD was expanding and buying up gallonage in Sidford and Exeter. Their distribution extended into North Devon, Okehampton and Sidmouth, and became a threat to the existing big three – Express, Unigate and the Co-op.

In 1991, Meadows Farm, a local farmers' group, who wanted them to process and package their organic milk for Tesco, approached EDD. At this stage almost all local milk was processed in Honiton and a percentage of total gallonage was sold locally through the retail trade. Any surplus milk from both Express and EDD went to Chard or Crediton for processing.

On 1 April 1993 a partnership was struck with Cricket St Thomas in which all processing of raw milk moved to the latter's factory at Chard. The EDD depot at Honiton became a distribution point for the enlarged Cricket St Thomas operation, but the Honiton milk factory remained as a dedicated, organic processing facility. With the demise of the Milk Marketing Board, the closure of the butter factory and the processing of liquid retail milk at Chard, the locally produced milk has to travel much further now.

Peter Hayward feels that the bulk farm collection around Honiton has gone through a period of inefficiency. As a result, all the retail milk sold in Honiton is now processed either at Totnes, Okehampton or Bristol, with a related considerable reduction in local jobs.

The EDD factory continued processing and packaging milk, but under a new label, Organics Ltd, for supermarkets. This facility and its associated businesses were leased to Horizon Farms, an American company, in July 2000 and remain dedicated.

The Highland Fling Café, High Street, c.1933.

Some draymen are seen in King Street outside Honiton Brewery, probably in the 1880s. The brewery covered some ten acres with stables, malt-houses and stores houses. The buildings were later demolished and the agricultural engineers Halse of Honiton occupy the site today. Some remains of the old brewery building can still be seen.

Left: *Workmen in the outer yard at Honiton Brewery in King Street pose for the photographer around 1880. The man third from the left was known as Grandad Major. He died in 1923 aged 91. The man seated at the front is George Long, a drayman who delivered beer to most of the pubs in and around Honiton. He liked a pint himself, so much so that he only got back to the brewery at the end of his round because the horses knew the way.*

Below: *Peter Halse of Halse of Honiton making a presentation to Bill Barber for his long service to the firm from during the Second World War to around 1975. Mrs Barber is on Bill's right.*

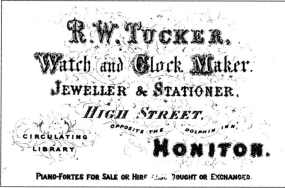

A party of Honiton builders and their employees on an outing to Cheddar in 1926. A halt that was made outside Gough's Caves for a photograph was almost obligatory for visitors to the Cheddar Gorge at that time.

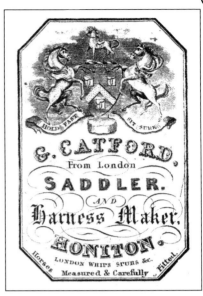

Right: *The senior members of Halse of Honiton. The agricultural engineers of West End, Honiton are seen here around 1970. Left to right, back row: Tony Sansom, Ken Martin, Malcolm Halse, Ernie Gardner; front row: Peter Halse, John Halse, Andrew Halse.*

A builders' outing from Honiton at, or on the way to, an unknown destination; judging by the fish and chip shop on the left it is possible that a midday meal break is about to be enjoyed. The pneumatic tyres suggest that the picture was taken in the later 1920s.

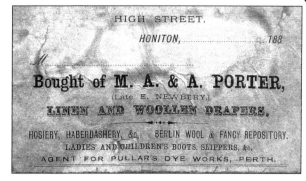

HIGH STREET,

HONITON, ...188

Bought of M. A. & A. PORTER,

(Late E. NEWBERY,)

LINEN AND WOOLLEN DRAPERS,

HOSIERY, HABERDASHERY, &c., BERLIN WOOL & FANCY REPOSITORY.

LADIES' AND CHILDREN'S BOOTS, SLIPPERS, &c.

AGENT FOR PULLAR'S DYE WORKS, PERTH.

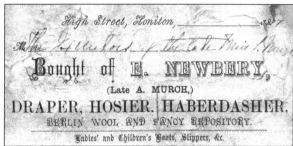

High Street, Honiton, ...

Bought of E. NEWBERY,

(Late A. MURCH,)

DRAPER, HOSIER, HABERDASHER,

BERLIN WOOL AND FANCY REPOSITORY.

Ladies' and Children's Boots, Slippers, &c.

HIGH STREET. HONITON.

F. F. BLADON,

WHOLESALE AND RETAIL

Linen and Woollen Draper,

and Silk Mercer,

(*High Street, near corner of New Street,*)

HONITON.

Harts of Honiton in 1986.

131

Above: *F. Studley & Son's new furniture removal van in 1946.*

Left: *An advert for Henry Langelaan, a sculptor of some repute who had his workshop next to the railway station. The advertisement has to be dated post 1908 because Langelaan is working on a model of a Boy Scout and the movement was founded in that year.*

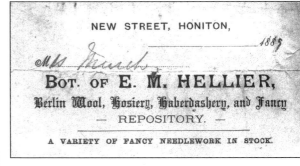

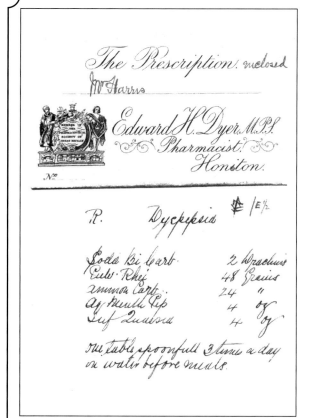

A LIST OF

FURNISHING IRONMONGERY

GOODS,

SOLD BY

JOHN MURCH, JUN.

HIGH STREET,

HONITON.

Agent for Spratt's Patent Dog Biscuits
and Poultry Food.

SAMUELSON'S LAWN MOWING MACHINES.

BENTALL'S CHAFF CUTTERS.

KNIVES, FORKS & SPOONS, IN ANY QUALITY,
LENT ON HIRE.

JAMES TOWNSEND, Printer, Gandy Street, Exeter.

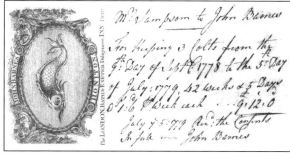

Above: *Local farmers getting ready to picket Honiton Market on 15 May 1970. If it were in France the High Street would be blocked solid from end to end with tractors and combine harvesters.*

Right: *The Environment Minister, Lord Belstead listening to Chris Sharland of KT Technology, Honiton, (fourth left) as he speaks about the firm's work in 1987.*

H.R. Harris, the High Street Pastry Cook and Confectioners, c.1920. Mr Harris, who was mayor of Honiton at one time, had two bakeries in Honiton. The one seen here was opposite the Dolphin; the other was in East End. His Central Restaurant, a visit to which was a must for the farmers' wives on market day, was advertised as being 'convenient for Visitors, Tourists, and Ladies and Gentlemen on business'.

Chapter 15
Firemen and Fires

Most towns in the nineteenth century had private fire brigades belonging to one or another of the myriads of insurance companies that existed. Honiton certainly had one belonging to the West of England Fire and Life Insurance Company and there were probably other insurance companies with brigades based in the town. The problem was that they only attended fires at the premises of their policy holder.

Honiton Town Council had purchased a standpipe for tackling fires by the 1880s and there were also at least two fire hydrants in Honiton. But the latter's main use seems to have been that of be that of watering the streets. On 16 April 1889, when it was intended to use them to damp the dust, it was discovered that, due to lack of use, they had become rusty.

In September of that year the Town Council expressed concern about the lack of a fire brigade following fatalities in an Exmouth fire. The town clerk said that there had been an Act of Parliament giving the council power to provide sufficient means of saving life in case of fire. The mayor, Alderman H. Hook, proposed that a fire brigade was formed and that an appliance (fire escape) be bought for around £50 and the fire brigade be drilled in its use. The purchase of an escape rather than a fire-fighting appliance probably stemmed from the line of thought that claimed that insurance companies' fire brigades did not operate to save lives but property. Indeed, when the board of guardians at the workhouse expressed concern about the possibility of a fire they were told that the building was mostly made of stone, little of which was likely to burn. No mention was made of the inmates' safety.

The council moved quickly, purchasing an escape capable of being raised 40 feet and also a jump sheet. Both were to be kept in the Swan yard. There followed an offer from the West of England Fire and Life Insurance Company that, as they were discontinuing their fire brigade in Honiton, they would be prepared to sell their fire-engine to the council on 'fair and reasonable terms'. Councils being what they are, Honiton Town Council replied that they would like to have the fire-engine if it was given to them, because other companies had given theirs to other places including Sidmouth. It is not known if the Town Council were successful in their attempt to get a free fire-engine, but they did obtain one and permission was given by the lord of the manor that it could be kept in the Manor House free of charge, under lock and key. The superintendent of the fire brigade (Mr E. White) and the captain (Mr F.B. Clarke) would have keys and others would be kept at the police station and at the Dolphin Hotel.

If they did get a free appliance they were not very grateful – within a year there were arguments over whether the West of England Insurance Company should pay for the fire brigade's attendance at the premises of their policy holder within the borough.

That fires were taken seriously was evidenced by a reward of £5 being offered for the 'capture' of an arsonist who set fire to a rick at Bramble Hill; a sizeable sum for the time. The expenditure of £56 for uniforms and £27 for a hose for the engine also shows the importance the council placed on having an efficient fire brigade in 1891 – the date of the brigade's formation.

By 1911 the old fire-engine had worn out and, in conjunction with the celebrations for the coronation of George V, the brigade received a new steam engine, purchased by public subscriptions. No doubt the fire that had recently gutted St Michael's Church had helped the council make this decision. The new engine was a Merryweather Greenwich that was purchased from the London County Council and could pump water 160 feet into the air, and pump 400 gallons a minute. The Merryweather did not last long – complaints about its inefficiency came to a head when it broke down on the way to a fire at Awliscombe. Rather unkindly, a tableau that year in Honiton carnival was on the theme of 'Two Hours to do a Two-and-a-half Mile Journey'. Before that, however, the entire brigade had resigned en-masse in protest and a new engine was quickly obtained.

By the 1930s the fire-engine was kept in the yard of the Dolphin Hotel but, in around 1950 when Alex Gosling was the station officer, the brigade moved to the purpose-built station at the end of Dowell Street. The first fire attended from there was at Sid Board's baker's shop in New Street, which is a computer-training establishment at the time of writing.

The brigade has continued to give loyal and valuable service to the town and people of Honiton and elsewhere. This was particularly true during the Second World War when it was often on duty in 1942 at Exeter during the raids that wiped out much of that city's centre. No effort is spared to get to a fire and put it out – in 1965 the firemen were taken to blazing outbuildings by tractor because of huge snowdrifts. In complete contrast a bakery fire at Stockland was so fierce that firemen had to contend with melted tarmac on the road.

Devon's chief fire officer, Alan Durrie, said at the Honiton fire brigade's centenary dinner in 1991, 'If the community continues to support us there will be someone here enjoying a similar evening in another hundred years.'

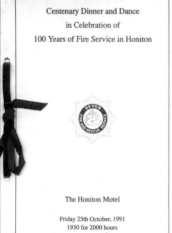

Above: *Honiton's new fire-engine makes its first public appearance on 22 June 1911, appropriately enough outside St Michael's Church, which had been severely damaged by fire less than three months earlier. The fire-engine in service at the time of the fire was not powerful enough and was replaced by the one seen here.*

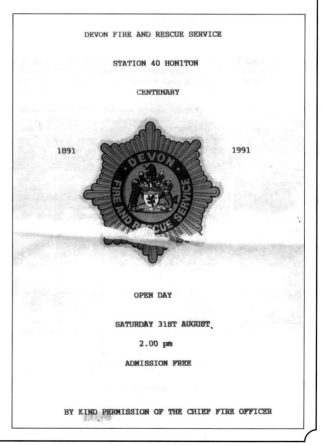

Mr A.F. Studley, Honiton's mayor, speaking to Mr Herbert Morrison, the home secretary, during an inspection of the Honiton National Fire Brigade on 30 December 1942. Mr W. Beer, the town clerk, is behind the mayor.

Many fires have gutted Honiton, notably those in 1672, 1747, 1754 and 1765. The plus side of many of the fires in the middle of the town was that several old hovels were destroyed and the handsome Georgian buildings, that grace Honiton's wide High Street, rose from the ashes to take their place. The fire of 27 August 1765 saw 115 houses destroyed, and it was claimed that the heat from the fire was so intense that it melted the church bells. St Michael's was the town church at the time, not the modern St Paul's in the town centre, and St Michael's stood (and still stands) above the town and over half a mile from the fire, so the bells would have been those of Allhallows Chapel. The chapel bells were recast and hung in the new church.

Robert Gidley, the Earl of Devon's agent in Honiton, wrote to Powderham (presumably to the estate manager) on 28 August 1765 as follows:

Dear Sir
This letter brings you the melancholy news of [a] great part of our town being burnt yesterday. The fire began at Mayor's the Blacksmiths (one of my son's houses) Mrs Cawley formerly liv'd in the higher part of the town towards the Meeting House and burnt down-wards towards New Street as far as Mr Guard's house, where Mrs Duke formerly lived and upwards on that side almost home to the Meeting House.

All the other side of the town including a back street is burnt down from Mr Gill's House up to Clapper Lane opposite the meeting house – the Steeple, Bells, School and School house are reduced to ashes – the body or Shell of the Chappel only is standing – Every Thing else in that whole space is in ruins – The Dispair of the People is inexpressible.

My Lord has had a great Number of houses burnt, almost the whole of the late Sir Henry Northcote's Manor is in ashes and [a] great part of my Lord's House. Those in hand are all insured except what was bought of Gibbons. I'm not satisfied if that is or not and very near the whole of these out on lease are also insured as I'm informed.

Pray speak to my Lord and every other Person of ability within your reach for some relief for those poor unhappy Wretches and send it over to us as is possible. We are now collecting from those who escaped the Flames for the relief of the poor Sufferers. I hope the Gentlemen of Exeter will be so kind as to make a speedy collection and beg you'd speak to some of them about it – I scarce know what I write. Therefore you must excuse everything amiss the Shindle-healing [?] saved all this Part of the Town on both sides. This Affair has thrown me back in the Gout of which I was before got almost well.
I am yours
Robt Gidley

Mr Garrett should fix with Mr Gearing when to come here & view the Damage my Lord has suffered which is

considerable in other of my Lord's Houses I hand which are not burnt down. I formerly left some of the Policies of Insurance with you at Powderham. Pray send them by Mr Garrett when he comes up that I may see the Particulars of what is insured & their Respective Sums the Houses are insured in.

St Michael's itself was the scene of a serious confla-gration on 11 March 1911 and was reduced to ashes. At the time the Honiton fire brigade was equipped with only a hand-operated pump and, although the outbreak was discovered in the early morning, it was not until almost 10.30a.m. that the firemen arrived on the scene. They were not slow or inefficient – but the system was. James Hurford, the sexton, spotted the fire and ran down the hill to the home of the captain of the fire brigade, Mr Tillotsen, and then verbal messages had to be taken to each individual fireman. When they arrived they found that the communion plate, brass, and other ornaments from the altar had been taken out of the church, along with the proces-sional cross and the altar cross, the pulpit desk, candlesticks and several brass oil-lamps.

They also found that there was virtually no water close at hand, the nearest hydrant being over 300 yards away and, due to the smallness of the main, there was no pressure. Attempts to dam a small stream produced a limited amount of water, just a few buckets at a time, and these were used in a successful attempt to save the tower. Help came from Mr Bate of Deerpark House who arrived in his motor car with a supply of Minimax extinguishers and Mr Banfield of the Dolphin Hotel sent up some more extinguish-ers. All were used to good effect, the belfry floor being flooded to a depth of several inches, and the fire was kept away.

The rector, Revd the Hon. F.L. Courtenay, tele-phoned Exeter for the steam fire-engine and the City Fire Brigade to be sent. That brigade's superintend-ent, Mr Pett, was at St Pancras Church when the call for help arrived and he quickly left for the fire station. He sent a four-horse steamer, the Devonia, with 15 men to Queen Street (now Central) Station, where a special train had been laid on and, a few minutes after 11 o'clock, the firemen special was on its way to Honiton. The line was cleared and the train allowed to travel 'at express speed'. It went to Blay's timber yard, which was the nearest source of water, but 1,900 feet of hose was needed to reach the fire. That meant that the steam engine could not pump with any force from the nozzle of the hose. The firemen got around this by erecting a canvas container on the church path and the water was pumped into this. The Honiton men connected to this and very soon two powerful jets where busy trying to save what was left of the building.

While the town was still basking in the afterglow of the coronation goodwill in 1935, the business premises

Honiton firemen at an unknown fire.

in the busiest quarter of town were 'threatened by one of the most alarming outbreaks of fire in the town's history, late on the afternoon of Monday 15 June 1937.' The fire began in the wine shop owned by Mrs W. Haynes and spread to engulf Mr Williams's chemist shop and Mrs Doble's ladies and gents hairdressing salon. A stiff breeze fanned the fire, which was thought to have started from a pile of burning rubbish near a small outhouse, and flames shot 20 to 30 feet into the air. At one stage there was considerable danger from drums of oil and spirit that had shattered in the extreme heat. Even worse was the danger posed by a 50-gallon drum of methylated spirit, the danger only being avoided when, with great courage, PC Hoyle and PC Dart dragged it clear with ropes.

Pulman's Weekly News reported that 'three of the four cubicles in the hairdresser's were burnt out... meanwhile [during the fire] a lady was having her hair permanently waved and was unaware of the danger.'

In the 1960s the home and baker's shop of Mr and Mrs Tom Lawrie was gutted in 'the worst fire in Honiton for many years.' Pumps and tenders from Ottery St Mary and Colyton assisted the two Honiton engines and High Street traffic was brought to a halt by clouds of thick, black smoke. During the fire a 62-year-old invalid needed oxygen after being rescued from his smoke-filled bedroom in an adjoining house. Glass shattered and slates exploded under the extreme heat but, despite this, around a dozen men and women helped move furniture from the house. Children helped as well, forming a human chain to carry sweets and many other items of food into another house.

No one was really surprised at the help rendered as that is what being a neighbour is all about in Honiton – and it was in a neighbour's (Mrs North) house that Tom Lawrie set up in business 'as usual' the next day, 'with help from his fellow bakers in the town.'

Another High Street fire came in March 1962 when the Devonia cinema was also gutted during an early-morning blaze on a Saturday. The fire broke out at 3a.m. and also threatened nearby thatched cottages on the north of High Street, sparks having started minor fires on several roofs by the time the fireman arrived. Soon after their arrival the roof and walls collapsed in a cloud of flames and sparks.

It would prove to be a busy weekend for the Honiton firemen – they had hardly returned to the fire station when they were called by radio to a chimney fire at Dalwood. Three hours after returning from Dalwood they were called to a grass fire near the Hare and Hounds on the Sidmouth Road. It took them over five hours to bring the 80-acre blaze under control, and during those five hours a second Honiton crew were called to a serious chimney fire at Lower Blannicombe Farm in Honiton Bottom, both crews returning almost together at midnight.

There was no let-up on Sunday when the brigade dealt with a chimney fire in the town, a common fire at Luppitt and, in the evening, a fire on the railway embankment near Wilmington.

Even fires sometimes have a funny side to them as Honitonian Eddy Marks found out (twice). Eddy, a fireman for 29 and a half years, was relaxing over a pint in the Dolphin Hotel after a cricket match when he was told that the fire station siren was sounding. He ran almost half a mile to the station, clambered on to the fire-engine and was driven at high speed to a kitchen fire – at the Dolphin Hotel! As it happens a fireman is not covered by insurance if he does not report to the station first.

That was in the 1950s. At another fire, this time at a tannery in Cullompton, and in pitch darkness, Eddy fell into a vat full of tanning fluid and was soaked from head to toe. He borrowed a pair of trousers to go home in but the dark brown fluid 'tanned' him as well, so much so that Eddy, a keen cricketer, could have played for the West Indian team until his tan wore off three weeks later.

New Street was closed to traffic on 21 October 1989 when firemen repaired the flagpole on the Town Hall. The pole was moving on its axis in high winds after a securing strap broke. The town clerk, Ivor Biddington, thought it was dangerous and called out the emergency men.

Chapter 16

Sport

Honiton Rugby Club

Honiton Rugby Football Club was formed in 1884 and played its first match at Budleigh Salterton that year. The result of the game is not known but included in the team were Major Lilley and Louis Wood, both of whom were still living 70 years later. A third member, who died in 1951, was John Roderigo who became a life member of the club. He was only 14 when he played in that first game.

The game quickly caught on in the town and, at first, there were as many as seven different rugby teams in Honiton. The town club fielded two teams, and the others were: White Stars, Scarlet Runners, Broomhills, United Choirs and Clarence, a side composed of employees of the old boot factory that was behind the site of the YMCA premises.

Honiton quickly became recognised as a strong club and included Exeter Chiefs, Sherborne School and Sidmouth on its fixture card. But the most fiercely contested game was the Seaton one – Honiton's local derby in which quarter was neither asked for nor was it given.

It was in the Seaton games that two Devon players regularly clashed. In the early years of the twentieth century Honiton had Revd P.L. Nicholas, a master at Allhallows School who went on to become the vicar of Drewsteignton. He was a member of the Devon team that won the county championship in 1901 and was capped three times for England in the following year. Seaton had Nobby Snell, who was capped many times for Devon and was once selected as reserve to travel for England.

The early away games were travelled to by a brake and horse that was driven by the landlord of the Dolphin Hotel, Harry Banfield, a playing member of the club, or one of his employees, Jim Neale. When they came to the steeper hills they had to dismount and walk. On one occasion, returning from Cullompton, a wheel bearing overheated and the team walked the last 10 miles home.

One of the club's stalwarts in later years was Dr D.D. Steele-Perkins, who also played for the Royal Navy and Gloucestershire and had a trial for England. He became a surgeon commander in the Royal Navy and was appointed to the staff of the Flag Officer, Royal Yacht. Other members that were capped at county level include Bill Brock, A. Woodr   )avey, W.E. Sprake, R. Nott, C. Be   G. Bassett (Devon and

Middlesex) and A. Carter (Surrey). In 1952 the club president was Dr J.E. Finlay who was capped six times for Ireland.

Honiton fell on troubled times at the beginning of the twentieth century and was wound up in 1902. Very soon however, Harold Carnell, a teacher at Ottery St Mary King's School, accepted a post at Honiton School and, thanks to pressure from the then president, Revd H.J. Fortescue, he re-formed the club and became captain. It was the start of over 50 years' connection with Honiton RFC as a player, secretary and treasurer. He held the latter post for 30 years until 1951, when he was made a life member.

The best years for Honiton were those between 1926–27 and 1929–30 when they reached the Devon Junior Cup final four years running. In the first final they were beaten by Paignton but won the next three in a row. Arthur Paull captained the first three finals and is thought to have been the only man in Devon to do so. After that they competed for the Devon Senior Cup.

In 1934 the club celebrated its fiftieth year with a game against the Somerset County team, which was held to a draw of three points each.

A typical team of that time was the one that drew 6–6 at home to Seaton in October 1936. It lined up: J. Stone, J. Cox, K. Hooper, E. Munt, D. Sinkerson, L. Gigg, C. Moore, C. Cottrell, B.C. Davies, S. Dommett, R. Lewis, L. Ackroyd, W. Boyland, C. Davis and W. Flood.

In 1952 *Pulman's Weekly News* reported that the record number of points scored for the club in one season was 124 by W.E. Sprague, a stand-off half just before the First World War. The previous record had been 110 by H. Chapman some years earlier. In more recent years the number of points awarded has been increased in some instances and that, along with a bigger fixture list, makes comparisons difficult. *Pulman's Weekly News* also recorded that it had been a great blow to local rugby when Allhallows School left Honiton for Rousdon in 1938, so many of the club's finest players having learnt the game at Allhallows.

In the opposite direction the changeover from football to rugby at Ottery King's School was a bonus – the school became regarded as the local nursery for the club.

The club had two very strong XVs in the years immediately following the Second World War; so much so that the second XV once went three seasons without defeat and the first XV met all the top teams in Devon.

Honiton Rugby Football Club in 1883/84, its inaugural season. Left to right, back row: *E.W. Hellier, H.H. Lilley, J. Wood, J. Stuart, C. Lilley, J. Sansom, D. Connett, C. Authors, Sgt-Inst Mackey;* front row: *F. Wood, F. Trace* (behind), *W. Bending, (captain) E. Edwards* (behind), *H. Denselow, J. Roderigo, J. Chard.*

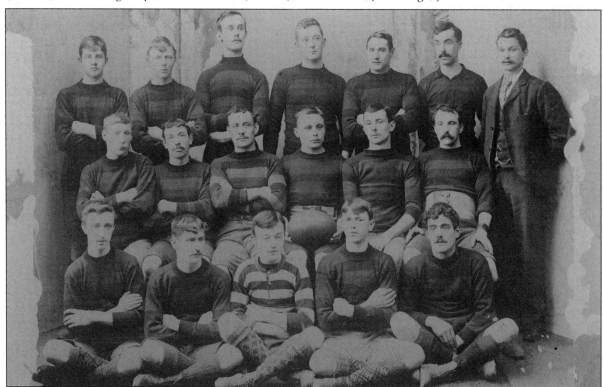

Honiton Rugby Football Club 1895/96. Left to right, back row: *A. Harris, H.W. Isaac, W.F. Tucker, C. Stickland, D.H. Hiscox, W.P. Bond, C. Ridge;* middle row: *F.R. Towell, F. Dobel, W. Wood (vice-captain), T.C. Ward (captain), E.J. Manley (secretary), J. Boaden;* front row: *A. Thomas, F. Wood, P.L. Harding, G.J. Isaac, J. Roderigo.*

Honiton Rugby Football Club pose outside Marwood House en route to Taunton in 1907. The driver of the brake was Jim Neale who worked for Harry Banfield, landlord of the Dolphin Hotel and a former mayor of Honiton. The players are (not necessarily in order): Fred Darke, Harry Summers, John Roderigo, Walter Vosper, Harry Howard, 'Whacker' Wood, Harold Carnell, Ernie Summers, Albert Cox, Frank Thomas, John Redfearn and Fred Pope. It is understood that the club will travel to Taunton in 2007 by a horse-drawn vehicle to mark the centenary of this photograph.

Honiton Rugby Football Club in 1911/12. Left to right, back row: E.J. Edwards, F.F. Edwards, W. Herridge, W. Thomas, E.R. Dimond (secretary), A. Dimond, F.W. Lane, A.F. Morrell (treasurer), H. Summers, R.J. Howard, J. Howard; middle row: W. Radford, F.E. Beer (vice-captain), L.G. Hearn, W. Summers (captain), J.G. Furzey, S. Woodrow, H. Rattenbury; front row: O.G. Shute, A. Tillotson.

Honiton Rugby Football Club, Devon Junior Cup finalists 1926/27. Left to right, back row: H.E. Carnell (treasurer), T. Dare, P. Trivett, F. Hayman, R. Martin, W. Baker, A. Chapman, C.N. Hatcher, W.S. Couldridge, P.V. Leresche (secretary); middle row: W. Baker, C. Selway, C. Doble (vice-captain), A. Paul (captain), A. Hoyles, W. Munt, A. Stone; front row: L. Isaac. L. Gigg.

Honiton Rugby Football Club, Devon Junior Cup winners 1928/29. Left to right, back row: H.A. Dunsford, A.S. Stone, W.J. Baker, A.T. Chapman, J.L.T. Rogers, H.W. Nott, W.A. Wyatt; middle row: C.M. Doble, A.G. Paul, A.E. Woodrow (captain), E. Munt, G.R. Lock; front row: S.E. Carnell, L.W. Gigg.

Honiton Rugby Football Club, 1994/95. Left to right, back row: *Jeremy Rice, Mike Harris, Mike Bowley, Dave Meadows, Simon Phillips, 'Knocker' White, Martin Allen, Dave Shepherd, Alex Bralsford, Neil Huggett, Arron Spence, Mark Vinall, Rodney Pidgeon;* front row: *Jamie Todd, Richard Woollacott, Nick Dicks, Nigel Broom, Bryn Small, Malcolm Salter (captain), Dave Wellington, Paul Vaughan.*

Suzanne Cricknell, aged 16, presents the shield given in memory of her late stepfather, Paul Spiller, to Honiton Working Men's Club A team's top scorer 'Buzz' Harris. Also pictured are Suzanne's fellow sticker-up, Susan Parry, and team captains Dev Fox (left) and Simon Bath.

Right: *Honiton RFC Annual Dinner held at the Angel Hotel in 1954.*

Honiton Rugby Football Club, 1951/52. Left to right, back row: *Reg Sprage (referee), 'Chippy' Stower (touch judge), Gordon Locke, John Lodwig, Arthur Long, David Pulman, Roy Miller, W. Hill, Pete Murray, R. Hill, G.R. Locke (trainer);* middle row: *J. Fowler, G. Fawcett (vice-captain), B. Evans, Jim Warren, Denis Hill (Hon. Sec.);* front row: *John Retter, Mike Kenwood.*

The decline set in during the 1950s, and by 1960/61, when Honiton failed to win a game, there was a danger of the club folding up. It did not – results slowly improved, support increased and, by 1974, the club was in a position to build its own clubhouse on a piece of land next to the playing-fields. The mayor, Councillor Hubert Black, laid the foundation-stone that year and by September Molly Jerrard, president of Bath RFC, officially opened the clubhouse.

At the time of writing the club continues to thrive and is in good hands. The future of the game in Honiton looks assured, especially after a Devon Junior Cup final success against Tavistock on 24 April 2004.

Honiton Rugby Club Representative Honours

England
Revd P.L. Nicholas was capped three times for England in 1902. He was a master at Allhallows School. D.D. Steele-Perkins (later Rear Admiral Sir Derek Steele-Perkins) had a trial for England.

Devon
P.L. Nicholas
W. Brock
A. Woodrow
E. Munt
W. Davey
W.E. Sprake
D.D. Steele-Perkins
R. Nott
C. Beer
E. Pike
S. Lewis
A. Bralsford
A. Hopgood
N. Huggett

Other Counties
A. Carter (Surrey)
L.G. Bassett (Middx)
M. Gill (Hants)
A. Dimond (Derbyshire)
C.N. Hatcher
E. Pike (Dorset & Wilts)
P. Dart (Dorset & Wilts and Eastern Counties)
D.D. Steele-Perkins (Gloucestershire and Royal Navy Colts)
T. Denne (Hong Kong)

Honiton Cricket Club

The early years of Honiton Cricket Club were probably humble ones, although the club soon flourished and played both the local villages and the bigger teams on a regular basis.

The Devon Cricket League handbook states that the date of the formation of Honiton Cricket Club is unknown, but it certainly existed in 1880 when reference was made to a game against Seaton. A map of 1880 also has a cricket field marked on it. This, however, was the field belonging to Allhallows School.

Almost certainly Honiton's first home was in a field somewhere behind Copper Castle, but in 1920, when the game resumed after the First World War, Honiton had moved to the Camp Field. They played their first game there on 22 May 1920 when Honiton scored 131–2 and then dismissed Royal Albert University College for 29 runs. Honiton's star was G.S. Napier who scored 74 runs and then took 6–12. Honiton's first postwar team was: J.A.H. Rogers, R. Hales, G.S. Napier, P. Levsche, H.E. Carnell, W.H. Barnes, R. Nott, H. Nott, P. Glaysher and A.E. Hooper. Two weeks later Napier was playing against Honiton for Allhallows School on the school ground. This time he scored 57, the school winning by three runs; obviously he was a master at the school.

The home of Honiton Town AFC and Honiton Town Cricket Club, Mountbatten Park clubhouse, is seen from the main entrance in 1992. It was formerly the sports ground for the Heathfield Army Camp.

The Camp Field was situated near today's Heathfield Park, but not actually on the site of the Army camp that arrived in the town some years later. It was on the opposite side of the road and some way past the Weston turning. It was called Camp Field because the Territorials used to hold their annual camp there. It was also used for football matches. A year after moving there the club left that field, the move being almost certainly forced on them because the owner of the field, Mr A. Davey, had offered it to the Honiton Union Agricultural Society.

Pulman's Weekly News (26 April 1921) recorded the location of the cricket club's next home when it was reported that, at a meeting of Honiton Town Council:

> Mr Carnell [the secretary] *had written asking the council to let them a portion of the field purchased as a housing site in Dowell Street for such time as building operations were in abeyance.*

The council agreed and appointed a sub-committee to meet the club, choose the spot and discuss rent. The first game at the new ground proved to be an historic occasion – Honiton, after scoring 97, dismissed Broadhembury for 33 with A. Woodrow taking 10–19, the first known instance of a Honiton cricketer taking all ten wickets in an innings.

Later, the club used the Allhallows ground and moved there on a permanent basis when that school moved to Rousdon. After the Second World War there were two clubs in the town – Honiton Town and Honiton British Legion. The town side folded in 1959 and its players joined the Honiton British Legion side. That club changed its name to Honiton Royal British Legion in 1971 when the Queen granted that worthy body the privilege of 'becoming Royal' to mark its fiftieth anniversary. Sadly, and with scant respect to an important part of the club's history, the Royal British Legion's name was dropped from the title in 1987.

The club's years of pomp were between 1994–97 when it won an unprecedented four East Devon Cricket League titles in a row. It had never been done before. Sadly, in 2005 the league no longer exists and it will never be done again. But, at the time (1994–97), the lace-town side were lords of all they surveyed and almost certainly the strongest purely amateur side in East Devon since the Seaton side of the late 1940s.

It was not always so. Back in 1901 the side was hustled away for just 18 runs at Bicton. Not the Bicton we know today, but a side of local gentry gathered together by Lord Rolle, the lord of the manor. Bicton was a posh place then and posh enough, even as recently as the 1930s, when the guests there included Edward VII (when Prince of Wales), George VI and his Queen (when the Duke and Duchess of York), the Princess Royal, the Duke and Duchess of Gloucester, and Mr Winston Churchill.

Honiton Cricket Club, c.1910, at the Allhallows Playing Field. Left to right, back row: *J. Roderigo, Mr Durbin, Mr Dommett, Mr Bassett, Mr Hussey, Harry Aggar (Allhallows School sergeant-major), Mr Hussey, H. Carnell (King Street Primary School master and organist);* front row: *Mr J. Dansom, Mr Deneslow, Mr Warren, F. Harding, ?. Mr Bassett and Harry Aggar would not have been allowed inside Lords in their braces.*

Honiton did not have anyone really posh in their team; their top brass was their president, a Mr Matthews, who was the mayor of Honiton. But they were posh enough to employ a professional, the only East Devon club outside of Seaton and Sidmouth to do so in 1901.

When Honiton were dismissed for 18 runs at Bicton, Lord Rolle's team went on to pass that meagre score without losing a wicket and, batting on, were finally dismissed for 190 after their number nine batsman C.E. Copleston hit a quick 59.

There was much enthusiasm over a suggestion that an athletics sports meeting could be held in aid of club funds. No doubt the attraction of such an event stemmed from the highly successful sports meetings run by Axminster Cricket Club at the time. It was also decided that the best fielder should be mentioned at the end of each season, as well as the best batsman and best bowler.

Low scoring was par for the course on wickets that knew little of groundsmen and even less of their ways, but some clubs were big enough, or rich enough, to employ a groundsman. On such grounds, Sidmouth, Chard and Seaton for instance, big scores were common enough. At Chard the home side scored 210 despite good bowling from Honiton's professional Gregory, who took five wickets for 52 runs. Honiton was bowled out for 70. Their team was: Revd J.H. Copleston, J.R. Ford, R. Kenwood, E. Hilton, K. McCaulay, J. Shortridge, E.J. Denselow, A. Woodrow, F. Clapp, J. Roderigo and W. Moore.

Honiton's ground was well maintained, as was Sidmouth's with D. Lambert (71) and J.F. Orchard (64) putting up 144 for the first wicket when Sidmouth scored 201–3 at Honiton a few weeks later. Honiton was dismissed for 56 by Bennett and Vizard who each took four wickets.

Honiton Town Cricket Club, c.1955.

Some of the members of Honiton CC who staged a comic cricket match in aid of a 1950s Honiton Carnival. Left to right, back row: Alec Gosling, Walt Pavey, Frank Pike; front row: Eddy Marks, Pam Atkins, Mike Strawbridge, Pat Leisk, Janet Pulman.

Somerset's Arthur Wellard with the bat autographed by the Somerset players that was used as a raffle prize at a testimonial match between Honiton Town CC and Somerset CCC in 1947. Left to right: Norman Mitchell-Innes, Arthur Wellard, Bill Andrews, Dave Pulman (Honiton skipper).

Left: Honiton Cricket Club dinner at the London Hotel, Ottery St Mary, in 1956. The picture includes: Mr Watson, Dave Pulman, R. Cann, Denis Hill, George Strawbridge, Joan Giles, Nigel Giles, Peter Toogood, Marion Gosling, Alec Gosling, Mrs Cann, Mary Pulman, Eddy Marks, Mrs Shobrook, Mr Shobrook, Mrs Strawbridge, Vic Strawbridge (president), Richard Whiteway (Whimple and Whiteways CC), Michael Kenwood.

Honiton Town Cricket Club, 1949. Left to right, back row: *Derek Le Cocq, Denis Le Cocq, Steve Harze, Mike Kenwood, Frank Pike;* front row: *Eddy Marks, W. Summers, Dave Pulman (captain), Jim Leisk, Pat Leisk, Pete Toogood.*

Honiton Community College Under-14s team, in 1994, which has had its most successful season in the Lords Taverners Colts competition. Captain David Lye is third from the right.

Back in Edwardian Honiton cricketers never bothered themselves with anything as common as league points, winning or losing draws, or changing the rules to stop a bowler bowling as many overs as his captain wanted him to (just because his pace put the wind up the opponents' batsmen). However, in 1910 the Honiton club did write to the MCC to solve a mild dispute that had arisen over a match with Payhembury. That summer had seen the club start with a debt of £2.7.4d. (£2.36p) being announced at the AGM. Total income had been £43.10.5d. The debt was considered satisfactory in view of some heavier than normal expenses and that there were some subscriptions still to come in.

The president, Cyril Tweed (the mayor), joint secretaries, Mr P.M. Hayward and E.H. Carnell, and treasurer, Mr Reeves, had all been all re-elected, Mr Carnell also serving as club captain.

The Payhembury game was the second of the season and the bowlers enjoyed it much more than the batsmen with 33 wickets falling for only 132 runs – the controversy came after the game. Payhembury made 44 and, after Honiton replied with 30, W.G. Harris who finished with eight for three, dismissed them for 22 runs. Honiton then scored 36–3 with E.H. Carnell who made 16 in the first innings and ten in the second, being the only man on either side to reach double figures.

Because the scores were level at the end of the game, Payhembury claimed a win on the first winnings, but Honiton claimed a tie. In the end, the matter was sent to the MCC for a ruling. That August the body's secretary Mr F.E. Lacey, replied that Honiton were right – under the MCC's law it was a tie.

Father and son were in opposition when Revd J.H.H. Copleston, who was the curator at Kilmington and played for their cricket team at the time, played against Honiton. The Honiton team included his son,

J.H. Copleston, in its ranks. Later, he would follow his father and become a man of the cloth. J.H. was one of J.H.H.'s three sons and a pupil at Allhallows School at the time. He put his pocket money in danger again when, after Honiton scored 115, Kilmington was dismissed for 38 with J.H. Copleston taking four wickets for 13 runs, the wickets including that of his father.

There was a tie when Axminster came to Honiton and both sides scored 46 runs. Honitonians to shine in this game were J. Hussey, who carried his bat for 28, and R. Griffiths who took eight for 13.

Edwardian cricket was the preserve of the 'better classes', and gaily bedecked ladies were regularly seen watching (and hopefully understanding) the game from the boundary. Games were often played in the grounds of the big houses with teas provided by the hostess (the staff made the sandwiches and cakes, of course). At Broadhembury, for instance, where Honiton scored 85–7 and dismissed Broadhembury for 15, Colonel and Mrs Gundry entertained the teams to tea at the Grange after the game.

Honiton Town Football Club

The earliest references to football in Honiton were made in *Pulman's Weekly News* when Honiton were reported as losing 3–0 at Beer in March 1920, but no mention was made of what type of game it was – league, cup or friendly. In 1922 Honiton lost 3–0 to Sidmouth in the Beer Challenge Cup, a competition that ran briefly in the early 1920s. This appears to have been a Thursday side that was comprised of shop workers who were unable to have time off for Saturday football. Although Saturday and midweek football do not easily mix, it seems possible that the Thursday team did play some weekend football.

Honiton Town AFC, 1956/57, the year they won the Grandisson Cup. Left to right, back row: *Dave Williams, Len Russell, Barry Pulman, Roger Atkins, Derek Evans, Cyril Pike, Brian Steel;* front row: *Richard Collins, C. Jeffries, Alec Gosling (captain), Pat Leisk, Mike Doble.*

That other football was played in the town is beyond doubt. The 1919–20 season was the first of the newly started Morrison Bell Cup competition, for which the trophy had been presented by the Honiton MP, Major Arthur Morrison Bell, for amateur teams in the constituency. The first final, in which Axminster Town beat Beer Albion 1–0, was played at the Camp Field in Honiton. Earlier that season Axminster had lost 1–0 to Alphington in the Football Express Cup final on the same ground.

In the summer of 1920 a move was made to start an East Devon League and, among some 20 clubs invited to a meeting at the Angel Hotel in Honiton, was the Honiton club. There was a suggestion that the new league could be split into two sections – eastern and western – and that the eastern section would consist of Axminster, Beer, Colyton, Honiton, Kilmington, Lyme Regis and Seaton. Axminster, Beer, Colyton, Lyme Regis and Seaton had already told the league that they were committed to playing in the Perry Street and District League for the coming season. Beer, a new club, said they would join and Honiton's spokesman Mr E.J. Denslow said, 'Honiton did not think there would be any difficulty in forming the new league. We have run a Thursday team and efforts will be made to raise a Saturday one.'

The move to start a new league proved to be unsuccessful. It would not have been able to call itself the East Devon League because a league of that name had been running for some time, and it came as far into East Devon as Budleigh Salterton, Sidmouth and Ottery St Mary.

But Honiton did have a football club and it held its AGM in September 1922. There was no mention of it being a Thursday side. One can only presume that the club played friendly matches – it certainly did not last long – the mayor, Mr S.W. Hook, accepted an invitation to be the president; the secretary was Mr V. Haynes, and the treasurer Mr R.J. Stickland. The committee comprised of Messrs J. Champerlain, J.P. Warren, J. Webster and R. Paul.

A rugby stronghold for many years (and it still is), Honiton did not have a town football club again for some years until it was re-formed in 1950. There was a Honiton British Legion team that was formed after the Second World War and competed in the Ottery and District League. Honiton's British Legion branch must have been an especially strong one, as it also ran a cricket club team. A report in *Pulman's Weekly News* stated that, at a meeting at the Star Hotel on Friday 26 May 1950, it was unanimously decided to form a Honiton Town Association Football Club. The mayor (Alderman W.J. Durban) was elected as the first president of the club. Many leading citizens of the town and members of the council, and the rector (Revd A.A. Fane de Salis), were elected as vice-presidents.

Right: *Fixture cards for Honiton Town FC (1955/56).*

Above: *Honiton Town AFC, 1984/85.* Left to right, back row: *Barry Burroughs (player manager), P. Brown, Martin Spence, Jeff Rayner, Terry Witt, Dave Palfrey, Craig Trivett, Jock McGrath, Mike Turner, (joint manager);* front row: *Andy Halman, Paul Ashford, Graham Charleton, Barry Dunn, Dave Salter.*

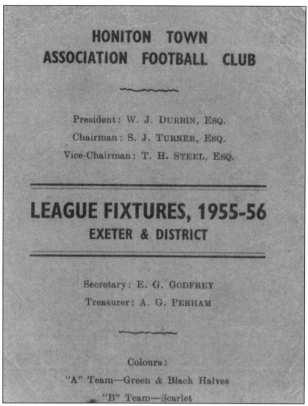

HONITON TOWN
ASSOCIATION FOOTBALL CLUB

President: W. J. Durbin, Esq.

Chairman: S. J. Turner, Esq.

Vice-Chairman: T. H. Steel, Esq.

LEAGUE FIXTURES, 1955-56
EXETER & DISTRICT

Secretary: E. G. Godfrey

Treasurer: A. G. Perham

Colours:
"A" Team—Green & Black Halves
"B" Team—Scarlet

The proposition was moved by Mr J. Underwood and seconded by Mr S. Lane. The Star Hotel was the new club's first headquarters.

Mr Durban said that they all wanted to put Honiton on the map, and a football club was one of the best ways. Mr G. Godfrey was elected as secretary and Mr J. Underwood as treasurer. The following were elected to the committee: Messrs G. Russell, H.F.C. Tucker, G. Hawkins, S. Quant, G. Leith, S. Vernon, T. Stamp, Taylor, L. Moore, C.T. Burgess, K. Randall, Hutchins, F. Stamp and A.G. Perham. The committee met to consider which league the club would join. Although Mr Venning, the registration secretary of the Exeter and East Devon League, addressed the founding meeting, Honiton Town spent its first three seasons in the now defunct Ottery and District League. At first, two sides were run but a lack of players, and fixtures, led to the disbanding of the reserve side. In the club's second season (1951–52) there was a playing strength of 14 players, with three members undergoing their national service, helping out whenever possible. Obviously, rugby was still the main sport in the town. The first captain was Bill Charlton who had been stationed at Heathfield Camp during the Second World War and had settled in Honiton; he had played for Farway for two seasons before the Honiton club was formed.

There have been many good players gracing a Honiton shirt through the seasons, none more so than Maurice Setters who played for East Devon Schoolboys and the Devon Youth side before joining Exeter City in 1953. He made his debut in the third division on 6 March 1953 in a 1–1 draw at home to Southend United. There were 8,392 at James's Park that day; not to see Maurice, but that was the sort of crowds City enjoyed 50 years ago. In the 1954–55 season he came into the league side in November 1954 and played in ten consecutive games (including one FA Cup game). Even in that short spell his talent was obvious and it came as no surprise when he was transferred to West Bromwich Albion for a fee, which was said to have been around £3,000. He was transferred again in 1960 for £30,000, this time to Manchester United for whom he played in the FA Cup final at Wembley in 1962–63 against Leicester City. His next club was Stoke City and then he played for Coventry City and Charlton Athletic.

His playing days over, Maurice was appointed as manager to Doncaster Rovers and was also at Sheffield Wednesday as a coach, Rotherham United as assistant manager, and Newcastle United as chief scout. At Sheffield Wednesday he was under Jack Charlton and, when Charlton gained the post as the manager of the Republic of Ireland's national team, he took Setters with him as assistant manager.

One of Honiton's biggest moments came in August 1984 when Liverpool played them at Ottery St Mary. A 3,000 gate had been hoped for but 1,200 was not bad. Liverpool, who included Chris Lawlor, Gary Gillespie, Phil Thompson, Bob Holder and David Hodgson in the line-up, won 4–0 after scoring twice in a minute to go 2–0 up after 11 minutes.

Honiton Royal British Legion football club at the Allhallows Playing Field in 1948–49, with the school canteen in the background. Left to right, the back row includes: *Mr Tinham, Alan Vickery, Tim Richards, Fred Cann, ? Pitt, 'Happy' Ashford, Arthur Long, Ray Cleaver, Mr Randle;* front row: *Les Moore, Jeff Gill, ?, Derek le Cocq, Denis le Cocq, Pete Murray, 'Chillie' Charlton.*

A Honiton youth football dinner. Seated at the top table are, left to right: *?, Gilbert Lovering, Mr Tucker, ?, Brian Steel, Ron Clayton, ?, ?.*

Honiton Bowling Club

The Honiton Bowling Club was formed in 1921, first playing on a 'lovely spot near the station that had been offered by Mr James Tratt of Pine Park.' James Hoskins offered to superintend the 'making' of the green and a Mr A.J. Redfern marked and levelled it. Mr Hoskins did a fine job and the embryonic and grateful club presented him with a pair of bowls. Thanking them, Mr Hoskins said:

Honiton is the chief town in East Devon but she lagged behind the others because it had no bowling-green, cricket field or tennis courts worthy of the name. We now have a bowling-green and perhaps other sports will follow suit.

On 19 November 1989 one of the finest indoor bowling-greens in East Devon was opened with the president of Honiton Bowling Club, Arthur Dimond, delivering the first wood. The four-ring green cost £250,000 and had taken four years to materialise after club members contributed around £50,000 in loans, as well as borrowing a similar sum from the bank. The East Devon District Council, Honiton Town Council, the Sports Council and a brewery all made grants towards the project. Mr Dimond said at the time:

It has meant a lot of hard work. We thought at first that the scheme was out of reach, but it was all made possible by the East Devon District Council buying the land and holding it for us. The site had been earmarked for development until it was discovered that there was no access.

Adjacent to the outdoor bowling-green off Streamers Meadows the rinks are on a par with those at Torquay and Paignton, and are probably the best in East Devon. The site was officially opened on 14 January 2000.

However, there were already a tennis and social club in Honiton, a reference being made to its fourth annual general meeting in April 1922 at which the subscriptions were 'slightly increased to meet the expenditure occasioned by the taking of a new ground.'

Honiton Golf Club

The Honiton Golf Club was formed on 14 April 1896, initially through the efforts of the mayor (Mr Nevill), and the club's history was extremely well written by Owen Cox in time for the club's centenary in 1996.

The original course was sited in the same area as the course in 2005, although the nine-hole course took up a lot less space. The entry in the *Golfing Annual's* Club Directory for 1896–97 records that the ground 'is 800 feet above sea level and about three quarters of a mile from the railway station.' Today's course is that far from (or close to) to the station and the modern clubhouse is around 820 feet above sea level. The nine holes averaged 250 yards. Plans were already afoot in 1896 to 'build a pavilion and a starting point nearer the town and to lengthen the holes.' History does not record whether or not the man 'employed as a groundsman one day a week's work for two shillings and six pence' (12.5 p) had an increase in wages when the holes were lengthened. The annual subscription was one guinea (£1.05p) and family tickets could be bought for two guineas.

The club's first president was the Rt Honourable Viscount Sidmouth, who held office between 1896 and 1904. Revd A. Marwood-Elton was the first captain and Mr R. Nevill the first secretary. The committee consisted of Messrs A.F. Bernard, A.T. Dunning, A.L. Gallie, Colonel Mackintosh, H.N. Pope and Cyril Tweed, a later mayor of Honiton.

Apparently the club did not own the land on which the course was situated because they were paying rent to a Mr Raddan, 'the tenant of the fields comprising the Links'. He had grazed cattle on the

Above: *Members of Honiton Bowling Club at the opening of a new season in the early 1950s watch an unknown guest bowling the first wood. Among those watching are: Tom Bambury (captain), George Doble, Bill Wyatt, Arthur Dimond, Archie Dimond, Mr Willcock, Jack Sansom, Bobby Clarke, Les Norton (chairman), Phil Embury, Bill Nickels, Harold Cottrell (president), Hedley Parker, Fred Mees and Ron Carter.*

Above: *A party of East Devon District councillors, led by chairman Ron Gigg (fourth from right), at the site of the new indoor bowling-green, showing them around is bowling club secretary Allan Nex (seventh from right). Arthur Dimond is third left. The gasometers in the background have since been taken down.*

Right: *Honiton Conservative Club B, Honiton Skittle League Division Four champions, 2001/02. Left to right: John Ritchie, Sylvia Marriott (captain), Gerald Clark, Eileen Clark, Roy Marriott, Rita Parker, Jane Pearcey.*

Below: *Honiton YMCA snooker team in 1947 when they were competing in the Exeter Snooker League. Left to right: Stan Sampson, Bill Major, Len Russell, Dick Drayton, Charles Selway, Bill Crane, David Pulman, Brian Canniford, David Pulman, Len Wood, Mike Bonetta.*

land and, for obvious reasons, this was unacceptable and caused the membership to drop seriously. This led to the club looking for a new home in 1904. Nothing was forthcoming and the club disbanded until 1922 when a meeting at the Dolphin Hotel on 12 July agreed that 'a Golf Club be formed'.

A nine-hole course was laid out by N. Lane Jackson, the founder of Stoke Poges Golf Club, on the same spot as the original course that was rented from the Combe estate. This meant that there were no problems with tenant farmers or their cattle. In fact, the club made money by renting the grazing (for sheep only) to Mr Ellett of Combe Hayes at an annual rent of £30. More cash was received by letting the rabbiting rights. A nice touch was that unemployed men in Honiton, who were paid for their labour, did the clearance and other work.

The first professional was W.J. Lilley, who also acted as green keeper and kept the club hut neat and tidy. In a male-dominated world Mrs Mills, the wife of a local doctor (and a member of the club), was the secretary until 1929, although it is stated later (1931) that 'the first Lady, Miss Dunning, was appointed to the Management Committee.' By 1931 a new clubhouse was built to replace a rather archaic Bow Hut, and in 1936 the course was lengthened to 18 holes. That year the club secretary, Dr D. Steele-Perkins, became the first person in the history of the club to hole out in one, doing so on the 124-yard sixteenth hole.

The Second World War proved to be hard on a club that was already having problems with membership. Petrol rationing meant that it was almost impossible to reach the course, even if one lived only a few miles away. The authorities requisitioned part of the course on which to grow potatoes or cereals. A bad first crop led to the land being left untouched until the end of the war, by which time Mother Nature had rendered it wholly unsuitable for playing golf on. With no small amount of hard work the land was returned to its previous golf-worthy state. A few years later (1953) a rent increase of over £50 to £120 led to the club buying the land for £2,200, a very wise investment and one that led the way to the club and course becoming one of the best in the area in 2005.

When peace returned in 1945 the course was again only nine holes, but this was increased to 14 in 1966 and to a full 18 on 7 June 1986, increasing the length of the course from 5,236 yards to 5,920 yards.

Since 1972 £110,000 was spent on facilities – the clubhouse was built in 1976, a bungalow was built for the steward, and further improvements were made to the course. In 1986 another £96,000 was spent on extending the clubhouse and improving the sewerage system.

Right: Honiton Bowling Club members as pictured in 1938 by the famous West Country cartoonist 'Stil', whose speciality was sporting cartoons for the Express and Echo *and the* Western Times & Gazette. *Among the members are Bob Delve, who ran the well-known Honiton electrical business; Archie Dimond, the printer; Jim Hoskins, the High Street draper; his partner, F.G. Pollard; Mr E. Hellier, the owner of Honiton garage; and George Cox, a local builder.*

Left: Judging by the absence of any mounted people this has to be a picture of the local Otter Hounds meeting outside the Dolphin Hotel around 1910.

Above: *Honiton's town centre seen from the air in April 1972 with St Paul's Church dominating in the foreground. Towards the centre background the old King Street School can be seen with, to its right, the Devon Lady factory on what was the Fairfield and is a housing estate in 2005.*

Left: *Black Lion Court, 1986.*

Below: *Work in progress in December 1986 on the shop development that would eventually become the Lace Walk shopping precinct and car park.*

An aerial view of Honiton in July 1985; the large open space in the background is now the Oaklea housing estate and the Dowell Street car park. The smaller open space towards the middle left is now the Cop-op precinct and car park.

Above: *Honiton MP Peter (later Sir Peter) Emery is seen outside St Paul's Church on 17 November 1984 at the launch of the Church Restoration Fund. Left to right: Peter Emery, Pat Allen (mayor), ?, Arthur Dimond, Edward de Cann (MP for Taunton), Revd James Trevelyan.*

Left: *An aerial view of Honiton taken in July 1985 and looking eastwards.*

Weston, the tiny hamlet to the west of Honiton, c.1910.

Above: The *Honiton photographer W.E. Berry wrote '... distribution of King George V Coronation Mugs by the Mayor Mr Seaborne Hook in 1911' on the reverse of this photograph. However, they look very similar to the mugs distributed to mark the signing of the 1919 Peace Treaty. Mr Seaborne Hook's mayoral years are no help; he was mayor in both years.*

Left: *Holy Shute House, Honiton, 1922.*

Below: High Street, c.1930s.

Left: *The East Devon District Council chairman Bill Thorne with Mrs Thorne, housing chairman Frank Lock and Honiton's mayor, Dr Terry Glanvill, welcoming Ray and Connie Dominey to their new flat in the Dunning Court complex.*

Right: *Leaders of the former Honiton Majorettes are seen handing over instruments to the pupils at Honiton Community College. The grown-ups are, left to right: Mr Larcombe, Christine Larcombe, Keith Joslin, June Pottinger, Mr Pottinger, Rosemary Joslin, Shirley Billett.*

Councillor Ron Gigg, chairman of East Devon District Council, and Frank Lock, chairman of the housing committee, are pictured laying the foundation-stone at the Dunning Court project in February 1989. Mrs Gigg is behind the stone.

Honiton's mayor, Ray Sharpe, launches the St Paul's Church organ appeal helped by the town crier, Joe Lake, and the rector, Revd James Trevelyan.

Axminster artist Ricky Romain is seen at Honiton Community College with some of the students. Left to right: Jenny Yeoman, Sarah Kellow, Ricky Romain and David Triggs.

Many people wanted the public toilets at the bottom of Northcote Lane to be demolished. The Express & Echo summed it up perfectly when they reported that they were 'A relief to many... but hated by some'. That was in 1992 – they are still there in 2005.

Right: *The mayor of Honiton, Joanna Bull, and Roy Cook, chairman of Devon County Council community services sub-committee, open the extension at Honiton Library. Bill Cogger, the chairman of Honiton Library Advice and Information Centre, and community librarian, Jenny Wood, are watching them.*

Above: *Bob Walker, mayor, with the town crier, Joe Lake, launching the Honiton Ring and Ride Scheme in March 1990 with disabled visitor Lilian Collins and Red Cross worker Jesse Norman.*

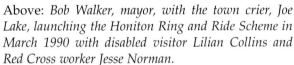

HONITON ART SOCIETY

20th ANNUAL EXHIBITION

at HONITON COMMUNITY COLLEGE
AUGUST 8th-18th, 1984

Open 10 a.m. to 7 p.m. daily except
Saturday, 18th August—close 4.30 p.m.

Chairman: Mr. GEORGE BLUNDELL

Secretary: Mrs. BETTY SCOTT
4 King's Court, Honiton
Tel. 41235

Treasurer: Mr. ANDREW COUSIN
4 Grantlands, Uffculme
Tel.: Craddock 40280

Honiton Primary School headmaster John Dalton is seen receiving a card and books about music on the occasion of his retirement in May 1986.

The winners of the 1980 Carnival Mastermind Competition were, **left to right**: *Cynthia Joy, Margaret Robson, Dr Catherine Glanvill and Linda Ward.*

Honiton Swimming Pool in 1988 during its construction.

Left: *A new sign went up outside Honiton on 27 July 1971. It is no longer there but, judging by the 'You Are Here' legend, it was just past the Weston turning.*

Below: *Residents and guests are pictured at the formal opening of Dunning Court in October 1990. Those present include Mrs Carol Gigg and Dr Catherine Glanvill.*

Honiton town crier Joe Lake with the scroll and mount designed by Stephen Wood in 1987, when Mr Lake competed in the first town crier world championships to be held in England.

Party at the Wesley Hall on 30 September 1954.

Subscribers

Graham I. Ayres, Offwell, Devon

Derek W. Blackmore, Offwell, Honiton

Mr F.C. Blackmore M.B.E., Honiton resident since 1927

Marie E. Bond (née Butter), Isle of Lewis

Michael and Shirley Bonetta, Otterymoor Lane, Honiton

Shaun and Tracey Bonetta, Mead View Road, Honiton

Edward J. Box, Yarcombe, Devon

Ada E. Brench B.E.M., Dunkeswell

Heather M. Burgess, Honiton

K.J. Burrow, Bucks Cross, Devon

Pat and Tom Burt, Honiton, Devon

David and Jean Cantle, Honiton, Devon

Jean E. Carter, Luppitt, Devon

Edna Chown, Honiton, Devon

Mr Brian R. Clapp, Honiton, Devon

Hazel M. Clapp

Mr W.O. Cleverdon, Honiton

Geraldine Coates, Honiton, Devon

Maurice R. Connett, Glasgow (formerly Honiton)

Sue and Norman Crampton,

John Dalton, Honiton, Devon

Diana M. Dark, Stockland, Devon

Timothy James D'Arcy Denne

Terry and Julie Davis, licensees The Three Tuns, Honiton

Leigh Colton Extence, Honiton, Devon

Anne and Terry Farebrother, High Street, Honiton

George and Barbara Fearn, Honiton, Devon

Ciaran Feeney, Honiton, Devon

Alan Freemantle, Honiton, Devon

Anthony Freemantle, Taunton, Somerset

Elsie M. Freemantle, Honiton, Devon

Mrs Wendy J. Frost, Honiton, Devon

Nigel Patrick Gigg

Mr and Mrs F. and M. Goddard, Adelaide, South Australia

James Goddard, Honiton, Devon

Thomas E. Gray

John and Joanna Harding, Honiton

Ross C. Harvey, Beacon, Honiton, Devon

Mr Stephen Harvey, Wilmington, Devon

Jean Hawkins, Honiton, Devon

Mr Allan Hayes, Honiton, Devon

Peggy Henley, Wilmington, Devon

Trevor Hitchcock, Honiton, Devon

Susanne M. Hoare (née Butter), Sidmouth

Samuel Hold, Dunkeswell, Honiton, Devon

Mr Barrie Kenneth Hooper and Mrs Janet R. Morrish, Honiton, Devon

Mervyn Hurford, Brockworth, Gloucester

Paul Hurford, Honiton, Devon

Mrs Susan Jane Jones, Honiton

Mr D. and Mrs M. Keitch, Clyst Hydon, Devon

Babs Knight, Honiton, Devon

David Lanning, Churchwarden of Feniton

Margaret A. Lapping

Patrick Lawson, Three Bridges, West Sussex

Robert Lee, 2005

Pat J. Leisk, Ottery St Mary, Devon

Mr Gerald Lewis, Exeter, Devon

Margaret Lewis

P. and A. Littlewood, St Brelade, Jersey

Roland Lock M.B.E., Honiton, Devon

Mr D.E. Logan, Honiton, Devon

L. Lowery (née Denne), Rockhampton, Australia

Mr Terry R. Lowman, Honiton, Devon

Mr and Mrs F.E. Martin, Honiton, Devon

N.A. Maxwell-Lawford, Honiton
Ron and Stella Miles, Honiton, Devon
Doreen Newton (née Bambury)
Winifred P. Nickels
G. and P. Northcott, Honiton, Devon
Tony Parsons, Crewkerne, Somerset
Margarett E. Pepperell, Thornford,
    Dorset
Mally Pickerell, Honiton, Devon
Cyril and Barbara Pike, Honiton,
    Devon
David Piper, Honiton
Dave Pulman
Melanie A. Quin (née Pulman),
    Honiton, Devon
Heidi P. Radford
Dave Rew
Jeanette I. Rice, Honiton, Devon
Michael R. Rich
Geoff Rickson
Y. Rogers (née Denne), Honiton, Devon
Clarice Shute (née Long), Honiton
Michael J. Shute, Honiton, Devon

Bob, Tina, Bethany and Zara Sillitoe,
    Honiton, Devon
Joan Smith
Derek W.L. Stamp, Weston, Honiton
Peter and Nan Steel (née Connett),
    Honiton, Devon
Mrs Patricia Thomas, Honiton, Devon
Ethel E. Trotman, Honiton
Brian J. Tyers, Honiton, Devon
Mary Wakely, Widworthy, Honiton
John F.W. Walling, Newton Abbot,
    Devon
Joy Walters (née Wensley), Hemyock,
    Devon
Mr R. Webb, Honiton, Devon
Judith Wheeler, Seaton, Devon
Pete and Chris White, Honiton, Devon
M. and L. Whitworth, Honiton, Devon
Heather Wicks (Rawride)
Lisa Jacqueline Wood, Andover,
    Hampshire
Michael Wood, Axminster, Devon
Pete Yates, Honiton, Devon

There are now over 140 titles in the Community History Series.

For a full listing of these and other Halsgrove publications, please visit
www.halsgrove.co.uk or telephone 01884 243 242.

In order to include as many historical photographs as possible in this volume,
a printed index is not included. However, the Devon titles in the
Community History Series are indexed by Genuki.

For further information and indexes to various volumes in the series,
please visit: http://www.cs.ncl.ac.uk/genuki/DEV/indexingproject.html